John Krause and Ed Crist

SUSQUEHANNA

NEW YORK SUSQUEHANNA & WESTERN RR

Front Cover: By May 1956, Susquehanna's fleet of RS1 road switchers had shed their elegant gray and maroon factory striping to sport an austere silver scheme with white diagonal stripes on the pilot, black lettering and black handrails. Combine is ex-Erie Stillwell type painted to match then new Budd cars. Crystal Lake depot appears in faded Erie green colors. Many NYS&W depots had been repainted in maroon and gray scheme following independence in 1939. Two car train from Butler was snapped around noon time by Hal Carstens on Kodachrome film, and who wishes he still owned the Studebaker Commander in Susquehanna colors.

ISBN No. 911868-38-0

Carstens
PUBLICATIONS, INC.

FREDON-SPRINGDALE ROAD FREDON TOWNSHIP
P O BOX 700, NEWTON N J 07860

Table of Contents

Acknowledgements

This book on the Susquehanna draws on resource materials from a wide variety of sources. The book's foundation lay in the extensive photographic record of veteran railroader Robert F. Collins. Bob further supplemented his photo coverage with a wealth of facts and figures on operations and equipment. Another treasure trove came to light as we examined the negative collection of Vincent Emmanuel. The negatives are now maintained by Railroad Heritage Press and we are especially grateful to Howie Samelson for their use. Vincent also added many facts and anecdotes to the record.

The list of photo contributors also includes such well known rail photographers as Rod Dirkes, Bob Yanosey, George Krumm, and Jeff Winslow. Winslow and George Votava also were able to shed much light on the Susquehanna's passenger roster. For factual material, we turned to our old friend Jay Diamond, who was able to furnish a complete set of the Susquehanna company magazine, the *Reflector,* published between 1947 and 1958. The *Reflector,* besides the usual social events and random events also furnished many historical facts and a contemporary record of the Susquehanna's most interesting years. Any history of the Susquehanna would also be impossible without drawing heavily on the late Walter A. Lucas' history of the road written in 1939 for the Railroadiana of America and which we hope will some day be reprinted. A rare book, we were fortunate to have the loan of it from Phil Simms.

Publisher Hal Carstens has had a long association with the Susquehanna and both furnished photos and encouraged the project. Carstens' staffers Jim Boyd and Bob Mohowski also both assisted in numerous ways. Tracking down the diesels brought calls to Don Dover of *Extra 2200 South,* Dave Hamley, Dick Marshall, and George Siliicott. Information on the railcars was graciously provided by officials of the Budd Company and ACF Industries, the Boston & Maine Railroad, Illinois Central Gulf Railroad, editor Luther Miller of *Railway Age,* and many individuals, among them Bill Price, Ray Hicks, William S. Young, Steve Maguire, John Stellwagen, John Scharle, Marvin Cohen, Carl Detwyler, and Ray Brown who in particular was able to clear up many confusing details of the leased and purchased Erie steam power operated by the Susquehanna. Additional assistance came from the New Jersey Zinc Company, the Hyper-Humus Company, to newspapers such as the *Blairstown Press, New Jersey Herald,* and *The (Bergen Evening) Record.* Susquehanna railroaders Bob Lentz and Charles Detrick were valuable sources of information, as were some of our old coworkers on the Lehigh & Hudson River: Jack Percival, Joe Spranger, and Bill Sisco. A longtime Susquehanna fan now living in Michigan also provided invaluable data: John Zuidema. Fred Heilich provided a complete set of right of way maps covering the Susquehanna's western portion from Butler to the Delaware River. We're, of course, indebted to the darkroom magic of coauthor John Krause whose technical skill eked every bit of detail out of forty year old drug store processed negatives. To all the above organizations and individuals, and to the many more we talked with, our sincere thanks in making this volume possible.

Edward J. Crist

John L. Treen

Susquehanna was made possible by many contributors, but one man stands above all others as the one who really "made" the book: John Treen. John hired out to the Susquehanna as a brakeman in 1946, fresh from high school and a hitch in the Army. He was not a railroad fan as we use the word today, but an amateur photographer who saw in his job ample opportunities for interesting pictures. He rarely reported for a run without his camera in hand and the result is a wealth of photos that were out of reach of the enthusiasts. As the years passed, John was promoted to conductor and became active in the old Brotherhood of Railroad Trainmen, now a part of the United Transportation Union. As a former railroader and union officer ourself, we think John represents the very best kind of enlightened, fair minded trade unionism and wish that the industry today had many more men like him.

As John's interest and expertise expanded, he photographed more roads, branching out as far as the narrow gauge lines in Colorado. John Krause and I have been pleased to use his work in earlier books, but of course the Susquehanna has remained his first interest. Just as important as the photos is John's amazing store of knowledge accumulated over more than thirty years of service on the S&W. Towards the end of the writing, we were bombarding him with almost nightly phone calls but he would invariably bounce back the next day with the answer. John's photographic skill and factual knowledge have been set down in print; yet we wish there was a way to convey more of his genuine liking for people and his sense of true friendship. We are pleased indeed to dedicate this book to a man who has excelled in both the industry and hobby of railroading, a fine person and good friend: John L. Treen.

Edward J. Crist

A BRIEF HISTORICAL PERSPECTIVE

The Susquehanna is an often maligned and even more often misunderstood railroad. To the younger generation, it is a shortline that pokes its way through the industrial clutter of northern New Jersey and occasionally ventures out to suburbia for a car or two. The older generation often thinks of the road only in terms of being the bastard stepchild of the Erie. There is a whole other Susquehanna that seems to have been overlooked, a road with a rich and diverse history and a unique character that survived the 40-odd years of Erie domination to blossom forth in the new independence of the Susquehanna in 1940.

To understand the beginnings of the New York Susquehanna & Western, it is necessary to conjure up a vision of New Jersey in the early years of the nineteenth century. The northeastern corner of the state was the manufacturing center of the United States, when the United States was still largely composed of the seaboard states. Pittsburgh was a frontier settlement and the coal deposits of Appalachia and the iron fields of the Misabe Range still lay undisturbed. Paterson was the center of the iron industry. Iron ore was mined throughout northern New Jersey and southern New York and native limestone and charcoal from the same region served to reduce the ore in crude stone furnaces. By the 1820's, charcoal was becoming a scarce commodity as the charcoal burners denuded entire mountainsides faster than nature could reforest them. The answer was found in the newly-found "stone coal", or anthracite, being mined in the Scranton area of Pennsylvania. The need to get hard coal from Pennsylvania to northern New Jersey would spark a flurry of construction, first of canals and later of railroads. Paterson's prosperity was insured by the arrival of the Morris & Essex Canal, completed in 1831. The M&E waterway received boatloads of coal off the Lehigh Canal at Easton and transported it across the state to Paterson and Newark. In 1832, the first germ of the future Susquehanna came to life when the Legislature granted a charter to the New Jersey Hudson & Delaware to build a rail line across the state from the Hudson River on the east to the Delaware River on the west. The project was conceived by a group of Paterson businessmen, but a combination of money panics and the existence of the proven Morris & Essex Canal prevented them from raising sufficient capital to

build the line. The charter was sold in 1857 to the Pennsyvania Coal Company, who actually ran a survey, but couldn't come up with the money either. In the interim; the predecessors of the Lackawanna, Lehigh Valley, and the Central Railroad of New Jersey were all pushing westward across the state, but far to the south of Paterson. Paterson had only the veteran Erie Railroad, which had not yet penetrated the coal fields.

With the coming of the Civil War, events began to accelerate. The war itself put a tremendous demand on the iron mills and manufactures of Paterson. This heavy demand was on top of a continuing growth that made the slow and seasonal canal a less and less viable source of raw materials. The close of the war finally saw the outbreak of "railroad fever", a uniquely American form of madness that would not subside for almost thirty years. The catalyst that would spark the building of the Susquehanna was not to be found in Paterson or anywhere in New Jersey, but rather 400 miles away on the shores of Lake Ontario at Oswego, N.Y. The Honorable Dewitt C. Littlejohn of Oswego had become a power in the New York legislature and he was going to see Oswego connected to the port of New York by a great midland route: the New York & Oswego Midland Railroad. The company had been incorporated in 1866 and was busy raising money and running surveys. Also incorporated that year in New Jersey was the Hoboken Ridgefield & Paterson, which intended to connect Paterson with tidewater at least. The year 1867 proved to be pivotal, as new companies sprang up and established companies began construction. The old New Jersey Hudson & Delaware finally began grading west from Butler in order to save their charter from lapsing. The New Jersey Western was incorporated to build west from Paterson, and in Sussex County, the Sussex Valley Railroad received a charter to build from the state line south to the Delaware Water Gap.

Of all these companies, there was no question that the New Jersey Western was the comer, the one which could raise the money and get the work done. Under the leadership of Cornelius Wortendyke, the NJW began building at Hawthorne in the spring of 1869. That same year, Wortendyke got together with Littlejohn and signed a lease giving the New York company a route through New Jersey to reach the port of New York. Construction of the Oswego Midland had begun in 1868 and was proceeding at a fairly steady rate. Wortendyke had the New Jersey Western

charter ammended to allow him to go right through to the state line, but the other existing companies had money, surveys, property, and grading already accomplished. It was more expedient to merge them all into one company and the spring of 1870 saw the formation of the New Jersey Midland Railway which was immediately leased to the Oswego Midland as the predecessor had been. The new company bought their first locomotive from the Rogers Works in Paterson to power construction trains. The next year saw a second locomotive purchased to work the completed stretch of track from Hawthorne to Butler. By 1872 the line was open all the way from the Erie at Hackensack to the state line at Hanford. Technically the NY&OM ended at Middletown, but they had leased the 14.5 mile Middletown Unionville & Water Gap to reach Hanford and connect with the New Jersey Midland. The MU&GW never reached the Water Gap of its title, but rather served as a feeder for the Erie and when it was leased by the Oswego Midland, it required a third rail to accomodate the standard gauge Midland trains, for it had been built to the Erie's six foot gauge. In the summer of 1872, the New Jersey Midland was leased to the Oswego Midland and construction of the last stretch from Hackensack to Jersey City was pushed to completion.

The great day finally came on July 9, 1873, when a train of flour left Oswego and travelled to Jersey City over the completed Midland route. The timing was terrible: the route was completed just as the Panic of 1873 was breaking out and in a few months, the Oswego Midland found itself in receivership. After the NY&OM suspended lease payments, the owners took their railroad back. Although through passenger trains continued to operate over the Midland route, freight traffic was going to the Erie at Middletown. A few more months found the New Jersey Midland taking over the lease of the Middletown Unionville & Water Gap, a property they would hold until 1913. In 1875 the effect of the Panic caught up with the New Jersey company and they also went into receivership. The receivers were James McCulloh and Garrett Hobart. Hobart later became Vice President of the United States under McKinley. For five years, the Midland struggled along while the bondholders slugged it out in court. Finally in 1880, the company was reorganized as the Midland *Railroad* of New Jersey with Garrett Hobart as president. The great Midland dream was gone; shortly the old Oswego Midland would become the New York Ontario &

Western and would get to New York City on the tracks of the West Shore. Like the dream, Cornelius Wortendyke and Dewitt C. Littlejohn both vanished from the limelight.

The Oswego Midland had been resurrected by an injection of fresh capital from established sources and likewise, a group of New York and Scranton money men decided that the New Jersey Midland was going to become a prosperous road by returning to their original intention of building to the coal fields. The moguls were getting more sophisticated at playing with railroads. It was the age of interlocking directorates and dummy corporations and all the tricks so dear to the hearts of Philadelphia lawyers. The New York and Scranton Construction Company was formed and they in turn chartered no less than *four* railroad companies to build to the coal fields. The principals must have decided shortly thereafter that they were being just a little too tricky, for the companies were only in existence for a few months before they were all merged with the original New Jersey Midland to form the New York Susquehanna & Western. The thought of building over the Pocono Mountains in Pennsylvania must have seemed like too much to bite off at one time, so the new Susquehanna was quite happy to let the well established Lackawanna bring the coal to Stroudsburg and the Susquehanna would take it from there to tidewater. With solid money backing them, no time was lost and passenger trains were running to Gravel Place (the interchange with the DL&W just west of Stroudsburg) by the fall of 1882. Then the coal began to roll. It's incredible to consider that even *four* multiple-track railroads could barely handle the torrent of coal that flowed from the Lackawanna River valley. After the years of struggling, the Susquehanna was becoming a railroad of substance and importance. By 1887, the volume of traffic required the laying of double track from Paterson to Jersey City. By 1892, the Susquehanna decided it was time to grab all the marbles for themselves. They were paying the DL&W 37% of the line haul and paying the Pennsylvania Railroad to deliver the coal the last three miles to the water, from Marion to Jersey City. To correct this situation, they chartered a company to build a line from Little Ferry to the Hudson River at Edgewater and bought up shore front property on which to build coal docks. The second and more ambitious project was the chartering of the Wilkes-Barre & Eastern to build a line from Stroudsburg to Wilkes-Barre. It took

HAROLD H. CARSTENS

less than two years to complete both projects and in 1896, the Susquehanna Connecting Railroad was organized to build additional lines up the Lackawanna valley to a point just above Scranton.

The continuing growth and prosperity of the Susquehanna could not be ignored by its larger neighbors and in January 1898, the firm of J.P. Morgan and Company began to quietly buy up the Susquehanna stock for the account of the Erie Railroad. The Susquehanna was formally leased by the Erie the following month and by July 1898, the operation was taken over by the Erie. In 1905, the first Erie locomotive was leased to the Susquehanna and relettered for the subsidiary. Erie locomotives would continue to invade the property until 1921.

In 1911, the Susquehanna quit the Pennsylvania Railroad terminal in Jersey City, moving to the Erie terminal in the same city. Freight was delivered to the Erie's Croxton yards rather than the PRR at Marion. The USRA operation of the Susquehanna during World War I, as with nearly all other roads under the government agency, nearly ran the company into the ground and the protracted shop strike of 1922 added

to the company's woes. Recovery was quick and in 1923, the Susquehanna posted the highest gross income of its history, roughly 5.5 million dollars. With the prosperity of the 1920's at hand, the parent Erie began to pour money into the Susquehanna, beefing up track and bridges along the line and introducing the famous Russian 2-10-0's. The Erie became a Van Sweringen property and the brothers from Cleveland installed John J. Bernet as the new president of the Erie. Bernet's short tenure is best remembered for the coming of the Berkshires and the transformation of the Erie into a hotshot freight road. He wrought a number of significant changes on the Susquehanna in the less than two years he held office. He ordered the bulk of the remaining Susquehanna engines scrapped and substituted Erie power. Likewise, the old wooden NYS&W coaches were retired in favor of Erie Stillwell cars and loco and passenger car work was transferred to Erie shops.

The bubble burst in 1929 and the throes of the Depression were made worse by the decline in coal loadings as anthracite lost favor to gas and oil. The other coal roads were also in bad shape, but they had the physical plant, the connections, and the motive power to make the switch over to an income based on merchandise freight. The Susquehanna, as a neglected ward of the Erie, simply couldn't pull it off. Floods in 1936 caused considerable damage and required a cash outlay the railroad could ill afford. Matters came to a head in 1937 when a series of first and second mortgage bonds came due and the Susquehanna simply didn't have the money to redeem them. The bondholders were not willing to wait for their money and on June 1, 1937, the Susquehanna filed Section 77 bankruptcy proceedings before the Federal District Court in Newark. It was ironic that the Susquehanna's old Midland Route partner, the Ontario & Western, had also entered bankruptcy just twelve days earlier in New York. The two roads had come full circle from bust to boom and back again to bust.

It only took the court four weeks to locate Trustees. The first was Hudson J. Bordwell, general manager of the road for the Erie, who died suddenly after only five months as Trustee. The second Trustee was Walter Kidde, a prominent manufacturer of fire extinguishers. Kidde represented a new twist in railroad bankruptcy cases: an outside businessman with no specific railroad experience. His first move was to terminate the lease of the Wilkes-Barre & Eastern, whose losses the Susquehanna had been making up under the terms of the lease. The WB&E then filed both its own bankruptcy petition and an additional petition to the ICC for complete abandonment of the line. The next move was a petition to cut one-third of the commuter trains off, which was done surprisingly fast. In the spring of 1938, additional commuter runs were discontinued and that summer, the operations of the vestigial Susquehanna Connecting Railroad in Pennsylvania were entrusted to the Erie. The WB&E was finally given permission to abandon its line and the last train ran on March 25, 1939.

In March of 1940, the break with the Erie was made complete when the Susquehanna opened joint offices with the NYO&W on the west side of Manhattan. The NYO&W staff had just moved from the more expensive offices near Grand Central Terminal and the new Susquehanna found it cheaper to have the O&W handle its office functions at first. Likewise, the O&W shops at Middletown were busy reconditioning the coaches and locomotives that the Susquehanna had leased from the Erie. Kidde was beginning to stabilize the road's financial condition and his purchase of new ACF railcars and the addition of new Paterson-New

York service was indicative of where he was taking the Susquehanna. In 1941, the last remains of the Susquehanna in Pennsylvania disappeared with the abandonment of the Hainesburg-Stroudsburg line. The Susquehanna bought their first diesels from Alco: RS1's and S2's. With the outbreak of World War II, traffic suddenly swelled and the Susquehanna was beginning to look up. Midway through the war, in February of 1943, Walter Kidde died. Those who thought Kidde could not be replaced were surprised when the court succeeded in locating a Trustee of equal caliber. Like Kidde, Henry K. Norton was not a railroader. He had begun his career as a lawyer and then switched to newspaper work, travelling all over the world as a special correspondent. Later he was variously associated with Armour, RCA, NBC, and Kidde's own firm. Having been executive officer of the railroad under Kidde, he was a logical choice to assume the Trustee's position. Norton brought in additional streamlined railcars and more diesels in 1943. By war's end, enough diesels had been purchased for the Susquehanna to proclaim itself completely dieselized, also claiming to be the first Class 1 road in the country to do so. The war's end brought the inevitable levelling off of traffic, but Norton was able to develop the Edgewater property sufficiently to maintain the Susquehanna's income. The equipment continued to be purchased: new diesels in 1947, Budd RDC cars in 1950, and stainless steel coaches in 1951. In 1953, the Susquehanna purchased their last order of RS1's and the company was formally declared to be reorganized by the Federal Court. Henry Norton continued with the railroad as president until his retirement in 1955.

Just out of reorganization, it must have seemed like a very cruel Fate indeed that visited the economic recession of 1957 upon the Susquehanna. The worst economic downturn since the Great Depression, the '57 recession had even the big roads nearly on their knees. The Susquehanna's old partner, the Ontario & Western, was finally abandoned and torn up that year. Desperate measures were put in effect in 1958: nearly all of the new stainless steel equipment purchased just seven or eight years earlier was sold off, cuts were made in the number of commuter trains, and the Hanford Branch from Beaver Lake to the state line was abandoned.

In 1961, the Lehigh & New England called it quits and the Susquehanna lost its westernmost connection at Hainesburg. In 1962, a new figure came to the

Susquehanna, a man who would dominate the road's image almost up to the present. Irving Maidman was a New York real estate dealer who had purchased some of the waterfront property at Edgewater and then proceeded to buy control of the Susquehanna, ostensibly to guarantee continued service to his Edgewater properties. Maidman's first move was to arrange a government loan for the purchase of three new GP18's. The ranks of the old RS1's began to dwindle and maintenance of both track and equipment was cut to a bare minimum. In 1963, Maidman became both chairman of the board and chief executive officer. In an attempt to unload the commuter trains, he made the unprecedented move of offering each commuter $1000 cash to quit riding the Susquehanna. Loyal to the end, only five commuters accepted the offer. Finally on June 30, 1966, the last commuter train ran on one day's notice. The next morning nearly a hundred stalwarts stood waiting for trains that would never come. In 1968, the newly-merged Penn Central offered to buy the Susquehanna, but the offer was turned down. The following year, traffic from Sparta Junction was embargoed ostensibly because a bridge near Sparta was unsafe. In 1971, a washout cut the main just east of the Jersey Central connection at Green Pond Junction. Shortly afterwards, the CNJ abandoned its track to Green Pond and the washout was never repaired. In 1979, Butler was the westernmost part of the Susquehanna still serviced. In 1976, the railroad defaulted on New Jersey taxes and was forced to seek haven in the courts once again. The aging Irving Maidman retired and Walter G. Scott became the new Trustee.

Whether the success stories of Kidde and Norton can be repeated again is pure conjecture. The property has been so severely debilitated that it will take long and hard work plus a large infusion of money to stabilize the Susquehanna's position. Many people feel that the deterioration which had taken place since 1964 leaves the railroad with no place to go but up. Despite its problems, the Susie-Q remains one of the few islands of independence in a sea of Conrail blue. It serves a growing territory and in a time of oil crisis, offers a tremendous potential as an alternative form of transportation for travel weary commuters who must rely on crowded roads in buses or private cars.

So come back with us to happier days when the plucky road cut loose from her mother Erie and set out to make her own way as the independent and very innovative Susquehanna.

MOTIVE POWER

When the Erie took over the Susquehanna in 1898, they found themselves with a good fleet of 70-odd locomotives, almost entirely 4-4-0's and 2-6-0's of both end-cab and camelback designs. After the lease was made, the Susquehanna bought virtually no more power on their own except that which they received from the Erie. It's important to remember that the Susquehanna legally purchased certain engines from the Erie which were lettered Susquehanna and leased others which retained their Erie markings. Likewise, the Susquehanna sold a handful of engines to the Erie and occasionally would lease one of their own locomotives to the parent road, but these were unusual cases. By 1938, all of the original Susquehanna engines were gone and when the road was cut loose from the Erie in 1940, the most convenient way to get new power was to simply lease the Erie engines that were so familiar to everyone on the road. Independence also brought a new trustee, Walter Kidde, who had no particular commitment to steam, for he had not been a railroader before. His term in the Trustee's position brought diesels, railcars and the streamliners. So let's take a look at the Susquehanna's fleet, a roster that in just a little more than ten years would undergo an amazing metamorphosis from nineteenth-century Camelbacks to stainless steel RDC's.

ROBERT F. COLLINS

ROBERT F. COLLINS

ABOVE and LEFT: Two views of the G-8 class Ten-wheelers, the 30 and 34 respectively. The Susquehanna 4-6-0's had originally been part of an order for 49 engines built between 1891 and 1896 by the Baldwin Locomotive Works and the Erie Shops at - of all places - Susquehanna, Pa. Between 1906 and 1916, twelve of the engines were sold to the NYS&W and used on milk and heavy passenger trains. The 30, 34, and 35 were reboilered in the early 1920's and this allowed two of them to escape the 1929 decimation of the class ordered by the Susquehanna's new president, John J. Bernet. The 35 died in 1929 despite its new boiler, and when 30 and 34 were finally retired in 1938, they closed the book on the long history of the camelback locomotive on the Susquehanna. Class G-8 4-6-0. Nos. 26, 27, 29 thru 38. Notes: Nos. 30 and 34 reboilered by the Baldwin Locomotive Works, 1922; sold for scrap, 7-24-38. No. 35 reboilered by the Erie shop at Susquehanna, Pa., 1920; scrapped at Meadville, Pa., 9-9-29.

RIGHT: Engs. 535 and sister 536 arrived from Baldwin in 1905, a more powerful version of a small group of Atlantic types purchased the year before. They were built coincidentally with the first of the 2500-class Pacifics to test the relative merits of the 4-4-2 and 4-6-2 wheel arrangements. In 1917, they went through the Hornell shops and emerged modernized and even more powerful. The 4-4-2's visited the Susquehanna very rarely, spending most of their time on the Northern Railroad and New Jersey & New York lines instead. When the photo was taken at North Hawthorne in 1940, the 535 was on a short term lease for commuter service and none of the Atlantic types was ever carried on the roster as a leased or purchased engine.

ROBERT F. COLLINS

C. GEORGE KRUMM

RIGHT: The freshly shopped 69 poses at Little Ferry in June 1940, only a few months after the breakaway from the Erie. A B-5 class 0-6-0 switcher, the 69 was part of an order for 70 switch engines placed by Erie between 1904 and 1912. Normally a steady customer of Baldwin, the Erie had a burst of generosity and split the order between the Cooke and Schenectady plants of Alco, the railroad's Meadville shops, and a relative newcomer, the Lima Locomotive Works. In 1912, Meadville built ten additional switchers, classed B-6 but virtually identical, and three of this group also plied the Susquehanna rails. 0-6-0 Nos. 69, 75 (Class B-5); 101, 104, 107 (Class B-6). Note: these locomotives were leased from the Erie in 1940 and never purchased, and were returned in 1944 after delivery of the diesels.

Two views of the chunky G-15b class Ten-wheelers, once the mainstay of the Susquehanna and Erie commuter pools. The 4-6-0's had come from Baldwin in 1903 and 1904 and like so much of the Erie's power, went through Meadville and Susquehanna shops between 1915 and 1924 to emerge rebuilt and modernized. Well known for its extensive stable of ugly engines, the G-15's were a welcome addition to the Erie's roster and even into the late 1940's, some of them still sported Russian iron jackets and brass plated hardware. Besides the Ten-wheelers purchased outright from the Erie, the Susquehanna also leased a number of them throughout the early 1940's. The G-15a class employed Baker valve gear while the G-15b's used Walschaert's motion, otherwise they were identical. 4-6-0, Class G-15a, Nos. 963, 969 (Purchased from the Erie, 12-1-44), 966, 970 (Leased, never purchased). Class G-15b, Nos. 953 (Purchased from the Erie, 12-1-44), 960, 961, 972 (Leased, never purchased).

ROBERT F. COLLINS

ROBERT F. COLLINS

Perhaps some of the best known commuter engines in the East were the K-1 Pacifics. A split order between Schenectady, Rogers, and Baldwin; the 59 engines (Nos. 2510-2568) built between 1905 and 1908 proved to be durable locomotives that were still providing excellent service right up until the end of steam on the Erie. The Russian iron jackets and cylinders are particularly evident in these photos. Combined with white striping on the drivers, rods, and running boards, and the brass hardware and red oxide cab roofs, they made an impressive sight at the head of a train of arch-windowed Stillwell coaches. The 2539 (ABOVE) carries a centered headlight, while the 2514 (BELOW) wears a high headlight and the brass and red round number plate. Although the Russian Decapods were the last operating Susquehanna locomotives, the last operation of steam on the Susquehanna was performed by leased Erie K-1's in the late fall of 1947, while the Susquehanna's diesels were laid up for their first major shopping. It was a very fitting way to close out the Susquehanna's 70-odd years of steam operation. Class K-1 4-6-2, Nos. 2514, 2539 purchased from the Erie, 9-30-43.

JEFFREY K. WINSLOW

JEFFREY K. WINSLOW

Both the Erie and the Susquehanna are well-remembered among railroad enthusiasts for the unusual Russian Decapods. The 2-10-0's were part of an order for 1230 locomotives for the Imperial Russian Government Railways made in 1917 and split among Baldwin, and the Richmond and Schenectady plants of Alco. About 200 of these engines were actually built before the Bolshevik revolution of November, 1917 caused the order to be cancelled. Faced with the prospect of unloading the oddball engines, the builders offered them at a low enough price to induce the Erie to buy seventy-five of them, numbered 2425 to 2499. The largest owner of the "Bolsheviks", as they were known, the Erie made good use of them and they proved to be the heaviest steam locomotives used extensively on the Susquehanna. Originally built for the Russian 5-foot gauge, extra wide driver tires allowed their use on standard gauge trackage, although they occasionally tripped over their big feet passing through switch frogs. There seemed to be more variations in front end arrangements, tenders, and other details among the Decapods (Greek for "ten feet") than in any other class of Erie or Susquehanna power. They couldn't be called handsome machines, perhaps intriguing is the best word; but the railfans found them an interesting curiosity and for the Susquehanna they rendered excellent service handling coal trains over the railroad's hill and dale profile. Class J-2 2-10-0 Nos. 2433, 2443, 2451, 2461, 2475, 2476, 2492, 2495 purchased from the Erie, 2-15-43.

Nos. 2435, 2445, 2490 purchased from the Erie, 12-1-44.

Nos. 2452, 2454, 2472, 2481, 2484 leased, never purchased.

Nos. 2454, 2472, 2481, 2484 returned to the Erie and sold, 2-8-43, to the Seaboard Air Line Railroad.

Nos. 2435 and 2492 sold for scrap in September of 1948; last operating Susquehanna steam locomotives.

ROBERT F. COLLINS

ROBERT F. COLLINS

The Susquehanna always claimed to be the first Class 1 carrier in the nation to completely dieselize and they began the process in 1941 with the purchase of the 231 and 233. The RS1 model had just been introduced that year by the American Locomotive Company and the Susquehanna's two units were part of a production of only 13 locomotives. Before the units could be delivered, the war broke out and they saw only a few months service in 1942 before being requisitioned by the government. The entire 1941 production of RS1's was rebuilt by Alco to six-motor units and shipped to Iran, where the Trans-Iranian Railway was struggling to keep Russia supplied with food and materiel during the German siege. The 231 returned to the U.S. later as a Navy unit while the 233 ended up on the government-owned Alaska Railroad. The government allowed Alco to resume domestic production in 1943 and a new 231 and 233 were built that year. These units could not be used as a multiple-unit combination, and by the Susquehanna's unusual numbering system were given odd numbers. All of the remaining RS1's had the m.u. feature and accordingly were assigned even numbers only. A 1944-45 order for eight units (230-244 , even only) completed dieselization and additional purchases in 1947 (248, 250, 252) and 1953 (254, 256) rounded out the Susquehanna roster of RS1's. ABOVE: The second 233 at Jersey City in 1948 sporting the original gray and maroon paint scheme.

Coincidentally with the purchase of the first RS1's in 1941, the Susquehanna also received six Alco S2 switchers (202-206, 208). The 1000-hp switchers rode on the distinctive Alco "Blunt" trucks. LOWER RIGHT: The 204 shortly after delivery. By 1979 only the 206 remained on the property.

In 1962, the Susquehanna was becoming desperately short of serviceable power and secured a Federal loan for the purchase of three GP18's from the Electro-Motive Division of General Motors. Continuing the even-odd numbering system begun with the RS1's, they were numbered 1800, 1802, and 1804. FAR RIGHT: The 1804 rides the turntable at the Little Ferry roundhouse.

ROBERT F. COLLINS   ROD DIRKES

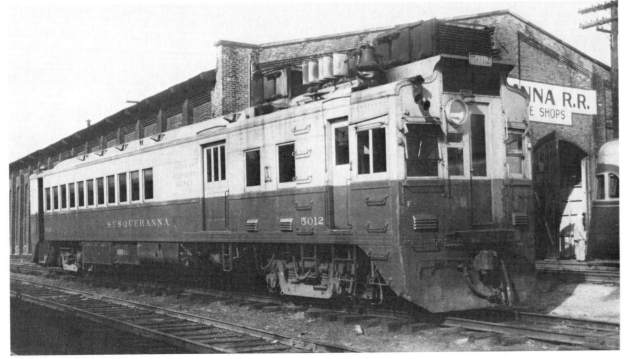

As a sharp businessman, Walter Kidde was looking for ways to cut costs and self propelled railcars seemed to be an ideal solution, for they were much cheaper to operate than an equivalent steam powered train. Had he been a veteran railroader, Kidde might have had some large qualms about the doodlebugs, but they did hold down costs and added undeniable spice to the roster despite their often erratic performance.

ABOVE LEFT: The very first railcars, and the only brand new ones, were the streamlined 1001 and 1002. Not to be outdone by the big roads, Kidde devised the tag "Streamliner" for the new cars, back in the age when it denoted the latest in rail passenger accomodations. The two cars were delivered by the Berwick, Pa. plant of American Car & Foundry in June of 1940. They sported a streamlined design, air operated center doors for quick loading, air conditioning, and the unique ACF pancake engine. The 290-hp engine was based on the patents of the Hesselman Motor Company of Sweden, but was built in the United States by Waukesha specifically for powering the ACF railcars. It was a semi-diesel design, employing the fuel injection principle of a diesel while retaining the ignition system and spark plugs associated with a gas engine. The low profile was ideal for mounting under the railcars and a hydraulic transmission furnished the variable speeds. The design was not without its drawbacks: the streamliners were tested for a very short period on the Hanford Branch, but could not keep the schedule on the heavy grades and so the steam powered mixed train was retained. The major failing of the pancake engines was their annoying proclivity for catching fire and this proved to be the undoing of the 1001. Running eastbound on January 20, 1946, from Paterson to New York, the streamliner caught fire at Passaic Junction and was totally destroyed. The Susquehanna eventually purchased four additional ACF cars secondhand and they are detailed on page 46.

BELOW LEFT: The 5012 at North Hawthorne, a leased Erie oil-electric car that came to the Susquehanna shortly after the arrival of the streamliners. The prototype car, No. 5000, went into service on the Erie in late 1930 and was a joint project of Westinghouse and the St. Louis Car Company, who built the body to the well-known Erie Stillwell design. The car employed two diesel engines in the front compartment and the familiar generator-traction motor arrangement used in conventional diesel locomotives and was apparently the key to their success in comparison to other railcars using single engines and various esoteric mechanical drive trains. They eventually grew in numbers through the 1930's and came to dominate the Erie's extensive branchline service. The 5012 was returned to the Erie in 1944 after the Susquehanna had acquired additional railcars and new diesels. It survives today at the Ohio Railway Museum in Worthington, Ohio, the only apparent survivor of the Susquehanna's self-propelled fleet .

ABOVE RIGHT: Apparently pleased with the performance of the railcars, the Susquehanna purchased additional secondhand cars during World War II. The 3001 was delivered to the Boston & Maine on February 23, 1926, as their No. 171. The J.G. Brill Company product was renumbered (August 3, 1931) to 1171 and sold to the Susquehanna on November 23, 1940. In this December 1940 photo, the 3001 has just returned from the Ontario & Western shops, repaired and painted in the two-tone red and gray Susquehanna scheme.

BELOW RIGHT: Motor Car 3002 was another secondhand piece that was built by Brill in 1929 for the shortline Cumberland & Pennsylvania as their No. 101. The little C&PA came under control of the Western Maryland and in the summer of 1942, the bigger road took over operation of the shortline and discontinued the passenger service operated by the C&PA with their railcar. Towards the end of 1942 or early 1943, the car was sold to the Susquehanna. Note that the 3002 was painted somewhat differently from the remainder of the Susquehanna's passenger equipment: the maroon extended all the way to the eaves on the sides and formed a shield on the beetle-brow of the car; the gray was used only on the roof. In this November 1943 photo, the car is still being used as a self-propelled car; sometime towards the end of the war, it was demotorized and used as a trailer behind the 3001. After the war, both 3001 and 3002 were displaced by additional streamliners and more diesels. They were finally sold in November of 1949 to the Ferrocarilles Unidos de la Havana in Cuba; we have not been able to determine if the cars still survive on the island's railroads.

ROBERT F. COLLINS

ROBERT F. COLLINS

15

Jersey City

The Susquehanna began on the shore of the North River opposite New York City at the Erie's Jersey City terminal. RIGHT: An aerial view of the terminal in the late 1940's. Ferries provided connecting service to Chambers Street in downtown Manhattan and further uptown at 23rd Street. The use of the Erie terminal was a fairly recent development. For many years the Susquehanna ended at West End, the connection with the Pennsylvania Railroad near the west end of the Erie and Lackawanna tunnels under Bergen Hill. Susquehanna passenger trains had rights over the PRR tracks from West End to the Pennsy's Exchange Place Terminal in Jersey City. Although the Erie assumed operations of the Susquehanna in 1898, the change to the Erie terminal was not made until 1911. That year the Erie opened the Bergen Archways, a massive four-track cut through Bergen Hill which replaced the old double track tunnel which was then relegated to freight service. BELOW LEFT: The morning mists are just beginning to dissipate as Train 920 from Butler pulls into Jersey City past the terminal tower on a spring morning in 1948. BELOW RIGHT: Ten years later finds the RS1's wearing a new silver paint scheme and heading up Budd-built stainless steel suburban coaches. The old Jersey City terminal is beginning to show its age and after the 1960 Erie-Lackawanna merger, all of the Erie mainline trains were moved over to the former DL&W station at Hoboken. However, Susquehanna and Erie trains of the old Northern Railroad line to Nyack continued to use Jersey City until the Northern trains were discontinued and the Susquehanna gave up all passenger service in 1966.

ERIE RAILROAD PHOTO, COURTESY MARVIN H. COHEN

JOHN L. TREEN

BOB YANOSEY

ABOVE RIGHT: GP18's Nos. 1802 and 1800 pause at the east end of Croxton yard waiting to deliver a train to the Erie-Lackawanna yard. The viaduct in the background carried the Susquehanna over the Erie tracks to a connection with the Pennsylvania Railroad at West End. A much older viaduct had been in service to perform the same function for many years before 1911, when the Erie took it over and handled the task of delivering Susquehanna cars to the PRR themselves. When the Susquehanna became independent, they continued to deliver Pennsy cars via the Erie, but the extra time required to move through the yards became unbearable and in 1951, construction was begun on the present viaduct and completed in 1953. Under the terms of the contract, the Susquehanna built the bridge and then sold both the viaduct and the trackage from County Road south to the Pennsy. The April, 1976 creation of Conrail made all this PC and E-L trackage one road and the old PRR connection was dicontinued. The viaduct still stands, shorn of its approach trackage.

BELOW RIGHT: RS1 No. 236 and two veteran Stillwell coaches cross over to the east side of the platform at Susquehanna Transfer for a return trip to North Hawthorne. The Susquehanna and the Northern Railroad of New Jersey paralleled each other from Jersey City to Babbit. The Erie Railroad had been chartered only in New York state and ended just above the state line on the Hudson River at Piermont. The Northern was built to furnish a connection and later became part of the Erie, although it is known by its original name to this day. When the Bergen Archways were opened in 1911, the Erie found that they had under their control two double track railroads and they instituted a policy of operating them as a single four track road. The Susquehanna was used as the two eastbound mains and the Northern became the two westbound mains. Even after the Susquehanna independence, the practice was continued right through to the early 1960's. The 21 miles of Susquehanna track from Jersey City to Riverside in Paterson was double-tracked between 1887 and 1891. In 1952, Centralized Traffic Control was installed between Little Ferry and Croxton Yard, perhaps one of the shortest CTC installations in the country and certainly unusual for a road of the Susquehanna's size. In this photo, the westbound platform between the Northern tracks is in the foreground, while the eastbound platform between the Susquehanna tracks is just out of sight in the tall grass at the right. In the background, a local freight heads east for Croxton. Just past the Route 3 highway bridge are the bridges carrying the Pennsylvania Railroad mains into the mouth of the North River tunnels to Penn Station in New York.

JEFFREY K. WINSLOW

RAILFAN: JIM BOYD

WARNING
PASSENGERS MUST NOT
TRESPASS BEYOND LIMIT
OF PLATFORM TO BOARD
TRAINS

RIGHT: An ACF railcar has just discharged its load of passengers at Susquehanna Transfer and the New York-bound riders are crossing over to board the Public Service buses that will take them right into Times Square. The streamliner will shortly cross over to the westbound side for the return trip and the engineer will only have to change ends for the return move, a distinct advantage of the railcars over a locomotive-hauled train. The Transfer was opened on August 1, 1939 and was one of Walter Kidde's innovations in upgrading the Susquehanna passenger service. The Lincoln Tunnel connecting directly with the 42nd Street midtown area of New York, had been opened the previous year and Susquehanna Transfer station was established to provide a direct service to the midtown area. It saved from 30 to 40 minutes on the time necessary to get to midtown over the more circuitous Jersey City-ferry-subway route previously employed. The year after the service started, an average weekday would see 18 round trips between the Transfer and Paterson City, 4 round trips to North Hawthorne, and 3 trips to Butler. The overhead bridge seen in the photo is the vehicular approach to the Lincoln Tunnel.

VINCENT EMMANUEL

RIGHT: Actress Lauren Bacall gazes provocatively down the length of the Transfer platform from the cover of the *Herald-Tribute* TV magazine. It's a summer day in 1956 and a westbound train is just leaving on the Northern tracks.

JOHN L. TREEN

18

RIGHT: A Russian 2-10-0, the 2451, heads a short stock train bound from Little Ferry to the packing houses at North Bergen. The location is Granton Junction, where the Susquehanna tracks joined those of the Northern Railroad. The J-2 is running on the Susquehanna's eastbound main; the westbound main swinging wide of the tower to make a connection with the Northern tracks. The tower was a manual interlocking that controlled the necessary crossover moves between the Susquehanna and the Northern. BELOW LEFT: George Krumm was at Granton long enough on this spring day in 1940 to catch the 2451 returning light with an ex-Erie wooden hack. The Russian Decapod is just beginning to cross over to the Susquehanna tracks in the background. BELOW RIGHT: Another short wait and railcar 5012 came along pulling a combine through the crossovers. The entire stretch of track from Granton Jct. to North Bergen was a photographer's delight: the Susquehanna and Northern on one side, and the New York Central and Ontario & Western just a stone's throw away on the other side.

C. George Krumm

C. George Krumm

C. George Krumm

ABOVE: Running full-tilt, the first of the streamliners, the 1001, is nearing Babbit station. The elevated tracks in the background are the New York Central's West Shore line and the Northern tracks have already crossed under the West Shore at Babbit station and are heading due north towards New York state. A close examination of the engineer's cab may yield an interesting surprise. When the streamliners were first introduced in 1940, the engineers got not only a thorough training in the operation of the new equipment, but the bankrupt company even sprang for a new set of white uniforms. The well dressed streamliner engineers were topped off with a white cap adorned with the S-in-a-circle Susquehanna herald.

Little Ferry

Little Ferry was the Susquehanna's principal engine terminal in later years and the site of a fair sized yard. When the North Hawthorne shops were closed in the late 1950's, all repair work was moved to Little Ferry and it remains the operations center of the railroad today. RIGHT: A look at the Little Ferry engine terminal in the early 1940's, just prior to the arrival of the first diesels. It's not generally known that the Little Ferry terminal played host to the Erie's famous 3300-class Berkshires. The renowed 2-8-4's were used on coal trains between Passaic Jct. and Little Ferry through the 1930's. After World War II, a leased Lehigh & New England Camelback was briefly used during the rush of export coal business to shove coal trains from Croxton to Little Ferry. LOWER RIGHT: An RS1 pulls a cut of cars off the interchange track at Little Ferry yard while an eastbound commuter train on the West Shore speeds east to Weehawken. An occasional respite from the procession of heavyweight West Shore trains would be afforded by the passage of an ancient camelback with a string of wooden coaches, an Ontario & Western train running on the West Shore. For a short period in 1883 and 1884, both the O&W and West Shore had used the Susquehanna from Little Ferry to West End while awaiting completion of their own Weehawken terminal.

VINCENT EMMANUEL

JOHN L. TREEN

ABOVE LEFT: A broad view of the compact facilities at the Little Ferry engine terminal. To the right are the shops and the back of the roundhouse, to the left is the storehouse and sand tower, behind the camera are the fueling facilities. The gentlemen at the right in the white shirt and hat, no doubt coming down to see who is photographing his domain, is Otto C. Gruenberg, the Superintendent of Motive Power. A mechanical engineer from the Midwest, Gruenberg began his railroad career in the locomotive department of the Milwaukee Road, worked for the B&M for some time and joined the design staff of American Locomotive in 1936. From Alco, he went to the Ontario & Western in 1940 and it was under his supervision that most of the Susquehanna's locomotives and cars were refurbished in the early days of independence when the Susquehanna shop work was being handled by the NYO&W at Middletown. In 1942, he left to join the Army and made quite a name for himself rebuilding the war-shattered railroads of the Phillipines. With the war's end, he returned not to the O&W, but to the Susquehanna as Motive Power Superintendent. In 1954, he was promoted to the post of General Manager and held that job for a number of years before his retirement.

BELOW, FAR LEFT: A close-up of the streamliner shed, sandwiched between the roundhouse and storehouse. The building was added to the Little Ferry facilities shortly after the arrival of the streamliners in 1940.

BELOW LEFT: Little Ferry terminal in the spring of 1977 shows how little it has changed in almost 30 years. To the right stands GP18 No. 1804, resplendent in a new coat of yellow and green paint. The original factory paint scheme has been slightly modified by doing away with the nose stripes and substituting a yellow wedge adorned with the well-known "S-ball" logo. To the left stands another freshly-painted unit, the Bicentennial RS1, No. 252. Despite the bankruptcy, the railroad and its people succeeded in getting the 1947 Alco repainted in what proved to be one of the nicer of the plethora of Bicentennial paint jobs. Local fans were elated when a steam cleaning of the unit prior to painting took off not only the dirt but all of the silver paint, exposing the well preserved original maroon and gray scheme.

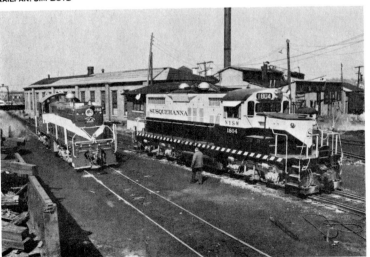

ABOVE RIGHT: On a spring day in 1949, the 2nd 233 races east with Train 912 from North Hawthorne, running neck and neck with an eastbound West Shore train. The yard tracks at the left were an expansion of an old coal storage yard built originally to handle coal bound for Edgewater. The construction of the New Jersey Turnpike across Little Ferry yard in 1950 took much of the yard property and in return, the state furnished a new yard west of the old one and much closer to the roundhouse area.

BELOW RIGHT: The new yard, looking north from the Turnpike bridge, was equipped for hump switching and became the Susquehanna's main yard, while the remnants of the old yard were retained for extra capacity. Right underneath the Turnpike bridge, at the midpoint between the old and new yards, is the switch leading to the Edgewater branch. The track leaves the main heading south towards Jersey City and climbs an embankment until it is high enough to swing towards the east and cross the main on an overhead bridge heading for Edgewater tunnel.

Edgewater

Edgewater is the aptly named riverside terminal of the Susquehanna, although the locale's old name of Undercliff seemed just as appropriate. Like the joint New York Central-Ontario & Western facility at Weehawken, Edgewater terminal was shoehorned into the narrow strip of land between the ramparts of the Palisades and the Hudson River, and was the furthest upriver of any of the New Jersey rail terminals. Edgewater was built to cope with the growing coal traffic produced by the extension of the Susquehanna to Gravel Place in 1882. By 1892, the coal was rolling out of Pennsylvania so fast that the Susquehanna decided it was time to have its own riverfront terminal

and they promptly organized the Hudson River Railroad and Terminal Company. Like the Lackawanna, Erie, and West Shore; access to the Hudson River from the west required a tunnel. Construction of the 5069-foot long bore began in the summer of 1892 and was completed in May of 1894. In the intervening year, the subsidiary company was formally absorbed into the Susquehanna and more importantly, the Wilkes-Barre & Eastern extension was completed. The 1898 lease of the Susquehanna by the Erie had little effect on the Edgewater operations. In 1912, the Lehigh & New England was given operating rights over the Susquehanna for their coal trains all the way from the juction at Hainesburg through to Edgewater, a practice that was discontinued by government order

during World War I and never reinstated. About the same time, the Susquehanna installed a car dumper that could handle twenty cars an hour, literally picking the entire car up and turning it over to empty it. The coal traffic took a steep dive during the early 1930's, but received a shot in the arm during World War II when the government ordered New England-bound coal to be handled by coast ships out of New York harbor and gave the Edgewater facility a priority rating. After the war, coal continued to flow through Edgewater, bound for Europe under the Marshall Plan. Finally in 1948, the coal dock was shut down and the dumper was sold in 1951 to the Reading to replace a fire-damaged dumper at the Port Reading terminal near Philadelphia.

HAROLD H. CARSTENS COLLECTION

ABOVE LEFT: A look at Edgewater yard in the late 1930's; the east portal of the tunnel is just out of sight in the lower right corner of the photo. We are looking south towards Weehawken and at the left can be seen the thawing shed for the coal dumper and directly behind it, the asssembly plant of the Ford Motor Company. The departure of Ford in 1955 to a new site was the first in a series of severe blows to the Susquehanna in the late 1950's and early 1960's. BELOW LEFT: A Russian Decapod, the 2443, prepares to leave Edgewater with a train of empty hoppers in 1939. Besides the yard tracks to the south of the tunnel, seen in the other photo, there were also yard tracks on the north side. An additional connection was made just south of the yard with a branch of the West Shore coming up from Weehawken. Edgewater tunnel had been double tracked right from the beginning and was something of a curiosity in that its west portal had been built directly under a cemetery.

HAROLD H. CARSTENS

HAROLD H. CARSTENS

JOHN L. TREEN

HAROLD H. CARSTENS

To most of the current generation of Susquehanna men, Edgewater is more synonomous with the Seatrain operations than with coal. Seatrain Lines contracted Susquehanna in late 1945 to install a terminal at Edgewater, but their ships were under government requisition. This delayed the opening until 1947, when Seatrain began operations, using its own loading dock. ABOVE LEFT: A view of the Seatrain pier from the New York side of the Hudson River. The large building to the right was the Hills Brothers coffee plant. ABOVE: A closer look at the giant gantry crane that swung loaded freight cars into the specially designed Seatrain ships. The Seatrain cars would be sorted out by destination in a special yard along where the old thawing shed had been. The cars would then be shoved, one at a time, onto a special cradle that sat flush into the dock. The cradle, complete with car, would then be transferred by the gantry crane into the hold of the ship, where the car would be winched off the cradle onto tracks in the hold. The ships had two destinations: Texas City, Texas, and San Juan, Puerto Rico; each about five days sailing time. There were of course, no railroads to speak of in Puerto Rico, but a small network of dockside trackage in San Juan allowed delivery of the cars. LEFT: One of the two small dinkeys used to switch Seatrain cars. The 150 and 151 had been built in 1942 for the Army and were sold to the Susquehanna in late 1946. They finally passed to an equipment dealer in 1960 and have remained an enigma ever since. One very definitely was sold to the Old Dominion Iron & Steel Company at Richmond, Va., but the fate of the other has remained a mystery. The Whitcombs had been replaced in 1958 by a new General Electric 45-tonner (No. 200) that eventually went to a mining operation in Quebec when the Edgewater facility was closed down. Seatrain moved their operations to the new Port Newark facility in the mid-1960's. The flexibility of marine containers and rising costs had killed the Edgewater terminal and dealt another body blow to the Susquehanna's sinking revenues.

Returning to Little Ferry, the Susquehanna tracks followed the Hackensack River for some distance going west. LEFT: Just leaving Little Ferry yard, the rails crossed the Overpeck Creek drawbridge and here an eastbound commuter train is seen approaching Little Ferry terminal in 1961. Just to the left the creek empties into the Hackensack River. The draw span is rarely used today although it is still serviceable. ABOVE; West of the drawbridge stands the Little Ferry station and a freight heading east is slowing down to drop off some of the crew at the station. The engine terminal at Little Ferry is inaccessible by car and nearly all trains would slow down passing the station to drop off or pick up crewmen. The man at the right is conductor John Treen, waiting to catch a ride down to the yard office and report in for a run. Little Ferry had been built as a passenger and freight station, but in later years was converted to freight only. It was typical of the stations along the stretch from West End to Hackensack. In the distance just past the Route 46 overhead bridge are the signals marking the end of the CTC installation that ran from Croxton to Little Ferry. Installed in 1952, the use of Centralized Traffic Control on such a small stretch of such a small railroad has always remained something of a puzzle.

JOHN KRAUSE

ABOVE: An eastbound train accelerating away from the station stop at Ridgefield Park. All along the stretch of track from North Bergen to Little Ferry, where the Susquehanna and the West Shore were within a stone's throw of each other, each road maintained a separate station. Such was the case at Ridgefield Park until just before the First World War, when a magnificent brick Union Station was constructed that served both roads. The Hackensack River lies to the left and what appears to be a road at the right is in fact the skeletal remains of the West Shore's four track main. Although the mighty New York Central went from four tracks to just one, the little "Squeak" next door still has its double track in place and the Union Station survives in a remarkably well-preserved state as an architect's office.

ABOVE: A Budd RDC demonstrator car heads east past the Bogota station in May of 1950. The demonstrator ran on the Susquehanna for two weeks and was so successful that the company put in an immediate order for four of the RDC1's. As the demo was strutting her stuff on the Susquehanna, the first units were beginning regular service on the Boston & Albany out of Boston to Springfield. The four RDC's were delivered towards the end of 1950 lasting until 1958, when they were sold to the Jersey Central. **ABOVE RIGHT: The 1002, one of the original streamliners from 1940, also approaches Bogota station heading east.** The signal at the right is unusual: the upper head is a conventional block signal, but the lower head is a smash board signal for the Hackensack River bridge. When the bridge was turned for river traffic, the lower blade would drop in place across the tracks and give a stop indication. Apparently the theory was that the sound of the crash would wake a sleeping engineer before he ran into the open draw. An identical signal at Hackensack protected the approach from the west. **RIGHT: A westbound commuter run on the Hackensack River bridge.** The coaches in the train were originally built for Boston & Albany commuter service, were later sold to the Delaware & Hudson, and came to the Susquehanna in 1960. The following year the ailing road sold the 16 Budd stainless steel coaches purchased in 1951 to Saudi Arabia.

RIGHT: A view of Hackensack station looking towards the east; just around the curve in the distance is the bridge over the Hackensack River. The smash board is visible in the distance, standing just about where the station would later be relocated. The impressive brick station at Hackensack had been built in 1901 for only $13,243, a price that seems unbelievable by today's standards. It was the only substantial brick station on the road, for nearly all the others had been built to the familiar NYS&W pattern of wooden frame depots. In later years, part of the large waiting room was blocked off into small stores and leased out to operators.

HAROLD H. CARSTENS

VINCENT EMMANUEL

RIGHT: An eastbound streamliner pulls into Hackensack station while two schoolchildren dutifully wait for the crossing gates to be raised again. We're looking diagonally opposite from the direction of the other view and the crossing watchman's tower in the background is a standardized relic of Erie days. Across Main Street from the station, the Susquehanna Tavern provided refreshments for the thirsty commuter.

ABOVE: In June of 1950, the Susquehanna opened their new Hackensack station, located two blocks east of the old station. Hackensack was the third of the old stations to be replaced in a continuing upgrading program during the late 1940's and early 1950's. The 230, a veteran of 1944, is seen heading east in 1960 past the new station with its neon Susquehanna sign.

RIGHT: Unfortunately for the railroad, River Street in Hackensack often lived up to its name and the new station was flooded more than once. In this November, 1950 view the water is only up to the curbs, but the fire department is busy trying to pump out River Street before it gets any higher. In the background, the new offices and plant of *The (Bergen) Record* are beginning to take shape.

RIGHT: The Susquehanna was becoming more suburban as it worked its way west through Bergen County. Here the 230 in the original maroon and gray scheme pauses at Maywood with an eastbound train trailing both a clerestoried-roof baggage-mail and a flat-roofed combine of Erie Stillwell heritage. The inset shows an overview of Maywood seen from the cab of a westbound freight.

BELOW LEFT: Streamliner 1002, making its way from Paterson City to Susquehanna Transfer as Train 824 is seen here in September 1948 accelerating away from the Rochelle Park station headed east. This area of northern New Jersey is much more densely populated today than it was in the postwar era, but passenger trains have disappeared.

BELOW RIGHT: In the fall of 1940, a glistening No. 2539 K-1 Pacific heads an equally shining consist of Stillwell coaches, all fresh from the O&W shops, west nearing Rochelle Park. The Route 17 overpass provided a fine vantage point to record the passings of the newly independent Susquehanna. Note in particular the well groomed double track mainline, a far cry from the 8 mph Susquehanna of today.

HAROLD H. CARSTENS   INSET: JOHN L. TREEN

JOHN L. TREEN

ROBERT F. COLLINS

31

ABOVE RIGHT: CNJ 1515 heads west past Passaic Junction station on October 17, 1955. The Fairbanks Morse H-15-44 is pulling a train of businessmen and railroad officials who are on a tour of northern New Jersey sponsored by the state and Newark Chambers of Commerce and an industry group known as the Newark Railroad Community Committee. Leaving Marion (the other name for the PRR connection at West End), the tour visited Little Ferry yard and ran to North Hawthorne before returning to Marion. The tour covered not only the Susquehanna, but the Pennsy, Lehigh Valley, Jersey Central, and the Erie. In the background, the 248 can be seen switching cars on the Erie interchange track. The Erie's Bergen County Line passes over the Susquehanna at Passaic Junction and for many years was one of the Susquehanna's busier interchanges.

BELOW RIGHT: Looking towards the west, Eng. 234 rolls east past Passaic Junction station with Train 910 from Butler. The RS1 sports the simplified maroon and silver paint scheme that appeared in the early 1950's. The coaches are the Budd-built suburban coaches delivered in 1950. In the background, the overhead bridge carries the Erie's Bergen Line over the Susquehanna. Just east of Passaic Junction was the site of the Coalberg Yard. Like the other anthracite carriers, the Susquehanna was faced with the problem of the seasonal demand for coal and solved it in the same way: by constructing coal storage facilities. The first "trimmers", or storage piles, were erected at Coalberg in 1901 and 1902. By 1906, ten trimmers were in operation with a capacity of a quarter-million tons of coal. After the decline of anthracite loadings, Coalberg continued to serve as a small yard for Passaic Junction and was finally obliterated by the construction of the interchanges between the Garden State Parkway and Interstate 80 in the late 1960's.

JOHN L. TREEN

JOHN L. TREEN

ROBERT F. COLLINS

C. GEORGE KRUMM

ABOVE: The date is September 18, 1940, and a shiny K-1 Pacific has just passed under the tracks of its former parent at Passaic Junction heading west. The track swinging off to the right is the 3.1 mile Passaic Branch running down to Garfield. Built in 1886, the branch still sees service.

RIGHT: The depot at Vreeland Avenue in Paterson, just over the Passaic River into the city of Paterson. The depot is a standard Susquehanna frame building and was noted among the Susquehanna stations for the unusual colored slates in the roof which spelled out "N.J. Midland" well into the 1920's. The old wooden building was finally replaced in September, 1949 by a new cinder block and brick structure very similar to the Paterson City station.

Paterson

ABOVE RIGHT: A pair of motor cars meet at the Paterson, Broadway station. The 5012, a veteran Erie gas-electric, stands on the Paterson City Branch, while a new ACF streamliner stands on the main. The first station at Paterson was a few blocks south of this location and was converted from an old barn in 1871. Despite Paterson's prominence at the time, it seems that its residents would not purchase sufficient quantities of Midland bonds and they had to settle for a recycled horse barn until the following year, when a new station was built just north of this location. The Broadway station was in the eastern part of Paterson and removed from the main business center of the city. To correct this problem, the Midland organized the Paterson Extension Railroad in 1881 to build an 0.75 mile branch from Broadway west almost to the Erie mainline at Straight Street. The branch involved some difficult rock cuts and was completed by the newly organized Susquehanna in the spring of 1882. The Broadway station was moved 500 feet south to the juncture of the branch and the mainline shortly after completion of the branch and for many years afterwards shuttle trains ran between the Paterson City station and Paterson, Broadway. The shuttles apparently were cut off sometime around World War I and the branch became freight only until the introduction of the streamliners in 1940. A second floor was added to the Broadway station in 1942 to house the offices of the car department, the superintendent, and the train dispatchers. **BELOW RIGHT:** An eastbound haul approaches Broadway station as the crossing gates hold the traffic on Madison Avenue. This is approximately where the old Broadway station stood before being moved to its present location. The second 233 is only three years old in this 1946 view and its gray and maroon coat still looks bright.

VINCENT EMMANUEL

JEFFREY. K. WINSLOW

LEFT: At the same location, just west of the Madison Avenue crossing, but five years earlier, K-1 Pacific No. 2514 was photographed sitting safely in the hole with a work train while an eastbound coal train rolls by. The workhorse of the commuter pools proved to be equally versatile at handling the most mundane assignments.

JEFFREY K. WINSLOW   VINCENT EMMANUEL

RIGHT: The first RDC-1 demonstrator of the Budd Company begins braking for the Paterson City station stop. The demos ran on the Susquehanna for two weeks in late April and early May of 1950. They were so successful that the railroad purchased two of the demos and two additional cars in October of the same year. The only perceptible difference in the demos and the delivered cars was the addition of a sheet metal pilot on each end, and the lettering.

RIGHT: MC 1002 pauses at the Paterson City station before beginning the return trip to Susquehanna Transfer. When the ACF streamliners were purchased in 1940, it was decided to reinstate passenger service on the Paterson City branch for the run to Susquehanna Transfer. The rehabilitation of the branch cost only $17,500, most of which was spent on constructing a modern brick and cinder block station at Straight Street. The Paterson City station was the first new Susquehanna station built in almost 30 years and its functional design inspired the later stations at Hackensack and Vreeland Avenue. Originally, a locomotive run-around track was provided in the event that the streamliners were displaced by a locomotive hauled train, but as seen in this 1946 view, it proved unnecessary and was barricaded. A portion to the left of the 1002 was left in as an industry track. Across the street, the Susquehanna rented additional office space in a commercial building right next to the old Erie mainline station. The drastic passenger train cuts of 1958 put an end to the Paterson City service and the branch was torn up a few years later. The sign shown in the inset, advertising the Susquehanna service at Paterson City, was typical of the aggressive advertising carried on during the Kidde and Norton years.

INSET: VINCENT EMMANUEL

HAROLD H. CARSTENS

RIGHT: A K-1 Pacific heads an eastbound commuter train on to the double iron at Riverside. The year is 1945 and steam powered commuter runs are just about over as the road continued to take delivery on new RS1's. The double track extended from Croxton to Riverside and it's something of an oddity that it still remains in place. Beyond the end of double track stood the Riverside Station, the fourth of the Susquehanna stations in the city of Paterson. Beyond the station, the rails crossed the winding Passaic River again to leave the city.

JOHN L. TREEN

North Hawthorne

ROBERT F. COLLINS

A neat and trim G-15b Ten-wheeler, No. 961, heads east out of North Hawthorne station with Train 920 on November 2, 1940, trailing a maroon and gray baggage mail and a dark green Stillwell coach. It's only a half mile to the Hawthorne station proper, where the Susquehanna crosses over the Erie mainline. It was here in March of 1869 that the Susquehanna first began to take shape when the predecessor New Jersey Western began construction at the Erie junction. The choice was a logical one, for the broad gauge Erie was the easiest way to obtain the supplies necessary to support the construction. The first Hawthorne station was located directly under the iron bridge that carried the New Jersey Midland over the Erie, but was later moved a half mile north. An interchange was maintained with the Erie at the Hawthorne station, although the great bulk of the interchange was carried on through the Bergen County Line connection at Passaic Junction.

37

RIGHT: Another polished and shining 4-6-0, sister 963, poses with a solid block of Stillwells fresh from the O&W shops at Middletown in front of the North Hawthorne shops, shortly after independence. The original New Jersey Midland shops were located further up the line at Wortendyke and were completed in 1872 as construction of the line was being pushed forward. A disastrous fire in 1891 leveled the old Wortendyke shops and they were never rebuilt. Instead, new shops were built at North Hawthorne in the spring of 1892, when the station was still being listed on the tables as North Paterson, a name it would carry until 1923. When the Wilkes-Barre & Eastern was completed in 1893, shops were opened at Stroudsburg, Pa. Shortly after the Erie takeover in 1898, the Stroudsburg shops were enlarged and all locomotive and freight car work was moved there from North Hawthorne. North Hawthorne continued to handle the passenger car work until 1929, when both North Hawthorne and Stroudsburg were closed in favor of the Erie shops at Hornell and Susquehanna. This complete lack of shop facilities explains why the Susquehanna was forced to contract all their repair work right after independence to the O&W shops. It took a number of years to reestablish North Hawthorne as a repair facility, and it served the Susquehanna well until the severe recession of the late 1950's forced the closing of the shops for all time.

ROD DIRKES

RIGHT: The year is 1960, and the shops at North Hawthorne have long been closed as the 230 leads an eastbound commuter run by the tattered depot. The depot had originally been located a quarter mile west of this site, where it had been known as Van Winkel, after the family who donated land to the railroad for the right-of-way and depot site. The railroad wanted to move the station closer to the center of North Paterson in 1891 and the family was understandably upset at losing their station. The Susquehanna decided to make the move on Sunday, May 24th, both to avoid delays to trains and to prevent the family from getting an injunction. The station moving gang no sooner went to work than they were arrested for disturbing the Sabbath and hauled up before the judge. The Super paid the $69 fine and then invited both the judge and sheriff to the nearest tavern for a round on the railroad. While the law was thus engaged, a second gang went to work and slid the station off its foundation and out on to the rails. A locomotive then dragged the building down the greased rails to its new location; arrests were made again and fines paid, but there was no free round of drinks the second time and the station stayed put in its new location. The building was leveled by a fire in 1976. The large brick structure in the background housed a firm whose principal business was making glue for United States postage stamps, a process which used large quantities of wheat flour. A few years before this photo was taken, a large portion of the building was destroyed by a dust explosion which killed twelve employees. A Susquehanna switch crew had just placed a car at the building and pulled up to the station for the next move when the building blew. The force of the explosion threw a loaded boxcar over and clear of both tracks. As the photo attests, the building was rebuilt to its original configuration after the disaster. Of all the railroad buildings in the area, only a small part of the old roundhouse still stands today.

JOHN KRAUSE

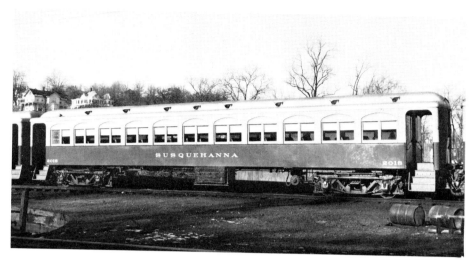

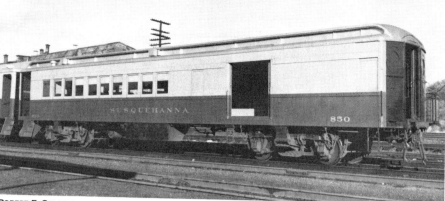

ABOVE LEFT: A broadside portrait of the classic Stillwell coach at North Hawthorne. The steel passenger cars designed by Lewis Buckley Stillwell remain one of the most distinctive pieces of rolling stock ever built. Stillwell was an electrical engineer and became involved in carbuilding when his firm undertook the design of the Hudson & Manhattan "tubes", the electric railroad connecting Newark, Jersey City, and Hoboken with Manhattan via tunnels under the Hudson River. Stillwell believed that in lieu of a heavy underframe, the car sides should share in the support of the car and he designed a unique trussed sideframe that did away with the heavy fishbelly underframes common at the time. When the tubes opened in 1908, Stillwell's new cars became the talk of the industry. In 1912, he designed what would become the classic Stillwell cars for the electric New York Westchester & Boston Railway, a heavy duty electric road running from the Bronx into Westchester County that died an untimely death in 1937. These cars featured the arched double windows and the rolled clerestory that instantly identify a Stillwell car. Erie president Frederick D. Underwood had been kicking around the idea of electrifying portions of the Erie since 1906 and he retained Stillwell to design a car that could be hauled behind a locomotive and yet be easily converted later to electric operation. Stillwell merely modified his NYW&B design slightly for the Erie and in 1915, the first seven Stillwell coaches and one combine appeared on the Erie. Eventually, the Erie would buy 398 Stillwell coaches and ten combines. The twenty-five cars (Nos. 2000-2024) sold to the Susquehanna were the oldest of the Stillwells, 72'-7" long and having eleven windows. Later Erie cars built after 1928 had an additional window owing to the 78'-1" length. Shortly after independence, the Stillwells were sent off to the Ontario & Western shops and returned in the new Susquehanna maroon and gray paint scheme, shown here. After the war, the cars were repainted in a simpler all maroon scheme and disappeared after the delivery of new Budd stainless steel coaches in 1951.

ABOVE RIGHT: The Susquehanna's three combines, Nos. 850, 854, and 855, were also former Erie cars, but not Stillwells as one might suspect. They had begun life as Pennsylvania Railroad PB-54 cars (for passenger-baggage, 54-foot). Like the Stillwells, the PB-54 group of coaches and combines were also designed for both electric and locomotive-hauled operation and the Pennsy built huge quantities of both types, while the Erie Stillwells never ran under wires. In the late 1930's, the PRR was selling off older equipment and the Erie purchased seven of the PB-54's, of which three were passed on to the Susquehanna.

BELOW RIGHT: An unusual sight: streamliner 1002 being turned on the armstrong turntable at North Hawthorne. The double-ended design of the cars, with operator's controls at both ends, usually made turning unnecessary. However, the engine was accessible from one side only and in this case, the car is being turned before a trip into the shop to facilitate the work to be done. One of the other distinctive features of these cars was the ability to convert the unused operator's compartment into a saloon on excursion trips. An ingenious arrangement of sliding doors and curtains made possible a mini-observation car, proving that they were indeed streamliners.

ROBERT F. COLLINS

JOHN L. TREEN

ABOVE: A J-2 Russian approaches North Hawthorne at restricted speed with a 36 car extra from the west. The signal at the left was the last to be seen heading west. Signals had been installed shortly after the Erie takeover in 1898, providing automatic block signalling from West End to Paterson, Broadway. The signals were extended to North Hawthorne in 1901, but west of there always remained manual block territory. Note the white flags on the smokebox of the 2-10-0 denoting an extra movement.

RIGHT: Being a railroader affords a photographer some unusual locations for picture taking. Working a Hainesburg extra in the spring of 1948, brakeman Treen steadied himself on the roof of the head car for a photo of the 252 and 246 grinding their way up the steep grade west of Midland Park station. The Susquehanna cut across a series of river valleys on its traverse of northern New Jersey and encountered steep grades over the mountains between. The road at this point is leaving the flatter area of the Passaic and Hackensack Rivers and climbing up to the summit at Campgaw.

HAROLD H. CARSTENS

ROBERT F. COLLINS

ABOVE: The 1802 trundles past the Wyckoff depot at restricted speed in deference to the track conditions, running light eastbound. The depot itself looks a great deal better than the right-of-way, for it is rented to a local women's club, who keep the building in paint and good repair. Regretably, most of the Susquehanna's classic little station buildings have disappeared entirely or stand neglected and decaying. **LEFT:** It's New Year's Day, 1941, and the failing light of a winter's day highlights the 2443 as it heads west with a BG Haul, smoking up the scenery just west of Wyckoff. Being a holiday, the Russian Dek has only 23 cars for the western connections. BG is the call sign for the Lehigh and New England connection at Hainesburg and as mentioned, the locals and drills on the Squeak were oddly tagged as "hauls". It might prove difficult to convince the younger generation that the heavily ballasted track seen here is the same mainline that they see today, weed grown and speed restricted.

HAROLD H. CARSTENS

ABOVE LEFT: Campgaw station in the summer of 1953; the summit of the grade coming west was surmounted about a mile before reaching the station. Campgaw remained open as a manual block station right up until the end of passenger service in 1966, but sadly was torn down later. **ABOVE RIGHT:** Only 1.1 miles further down the grade stood the neat and trim Crystal Lake station. The building poking through the trees behind the station is the Crystal Lake Inn, which once accomodated picnickers and bathers who would ride the

HAROLD H. CARSTENS

Susquehanna from Paterson. Crystal Lake was man made and disappeared during the mid-1950's when the dam containing it finally collapsed. The station survived to the mid-1960's, although it had not an agent for many, many years. Slightly downgrade from the station near the lake itself, the Susquehanna once had a water station, a seemingly awkward place to stop for water for it was right in the middle of the worst part of the grade.

RIGHT: The 232 heads Train 924 from Butler east up the grade out of Oakland in the summer of 1953. The photo also records an extremely unusual occurence on the Susquehanna: the 232 is carrying green flags for a second section! That doesn't indicate a swell of commuters, but rather Budd car M-1 carrying an officer's special which the dispatcher has decided to run as 2nd 924. One can imagine the trainmen on adjacent roads further east scratching their heads and trying to figure out why the little Susquehanna is running their trains in sections. The stiff grade out of the Ramapo River valley extended for roughly four miles from Oakland up to Campgaw. The Oakland station was the last of the Susquehanna stations to be replaced. A joint agreement was worked out between officials of the Post Office, the Borough of Oakland, and the railroad, whereby the station grounds were sold to the Post Office for a new building which contained a ticket window for the railroad in addition to the postal facilities. The lobby of the post office was also to serve as the waiting room, apparently the first time that the P.O. had ever made such an arrangement with a railroad. The Borough chipped in and provided commuter parking on the site of the old freight yards west of the station. The unusual project was completed in the spring of 1958, ironically just after two-thirds of the passenger trains had been cut off.

JOHN L. TREEN

HAROLD H. CARSTENS

BOB YANOSEY

ABOVE: The 231 is silhouetted on the Ramapo River bridge, trailing but a single ex-D&H coach on December 29, 1965. The New Year is a few days away, a year that will see the end of the Susquehanna passenger service. Just east of the bridge, a long passing track extends right up to the Oakland station, which survives today as the borough post office, although with no indication of its former use as a rail station.

RIGHT: This diminutive shelter at West Oakland served the needs of the people on the west bank of the Ramapo. The bucolic nature of the photo belies the activity once seen here in the days when the Susquehanna was moving mountains of anthracite to tidewater. The view looks east towards the river. A few hundred feet back behind the camera to the west was the end of a long passing track know as the Brickyard Switch. None of the natives could ever recall a brickyard anywhere remotely close to this area. Across the main from the passing track was another short spur which held the pusher engines assigned to assist eastbound coal trains up the steep grade to Campgaw. The coal trains would come roaring downhill towards the river without slacking their speed. Once the caboose cleared the switch, the brakeman would quickly throw it over and the pusher engine would take off to catch up with the coal drag. The coupling was made on the fly, the amenities of tying in the air brakes were dispensed with, and the pusher would simply hang right on, shoving all the way to the summit. The practice was continued for many years, apparently without any incidents, but we can be sure that today's officials would have a fit of apoplexy at the mere mention of such a move.

INSET: ED CRIST   JOHN KRAUSE   JOHN L. TREEN

ABOVE: The company picnic train heads west past Pompton Lakes station in August ,1951. The Susquehanna Outings, as the specials were known , were run for many years from Jersey City to Blairstown Airport, where the picnic was held. Stops were made only at Little Ferry, Paterson, and North Hawthorne to pick up employees, so the 236 is rolling right past the waiting commuters. East of the station, the large explosives plant of the DuPont company furnished a heavy business to the Susquehanna. A more unusual form of business appeared from time to time in the form of the hordes of people descending upon Pompton Lakes to watch the training of championship boxers at the famed camp of Dr. Joseph N. Bier. Established in the early 1920's, the camp was training grounds for nearly every champ who stepped in the ring for almost thirty years. The station at Pompton Lakes is a beautiful structure of uncoursed granite rubble and survives today (INSET) as an office building. It was designed and built in 1928 by an architectural firm from nearby Midvale, and closely resembles a number of other mainline and branchline Erie stations of the same period.

RIGHT: A westbound Butler train pulls away from the Pompton Lakes station in 1961, trailing but a single coach. Crossing the Wanaque River, the Pompton Junction diamond lies just ahead, where the NYS&W will cross yet another Erie line, the Greenwood Lake branch. The entire Pompton Lakes area, located at the confluence of the Pequannock, Wanaque, and Ramapo Rivers, has a very old history and was once a leader in New Jersey's iron industry. A forge on the Ramapo produced both cannons and balls that were drawn over the famed Cannonball Road to support the defense of West Point during the American Revolution.

44

ABOVE LEFT: An Erie RS3 approaches Pompton Junction from the south with a string of Stillwell's in the late 1950's; the 913 is only a few hundred feet away from hitting the diamond. In the early decades of this century, Pompton Junction was protected by an ornate Erie signal tower. The tower disappeared sometime around 1930 to be replaced by automatic interlocking signals; signals were located in both directions on both lines and the first train to hit the circuit got the clear indication. Originally known as the Montclair Railway, this line was once a prime contender with the New Jersey Midland for becoming the southern connection of the Oswego Midland. The company was in such horrid financial shape and would have required a tunnel to effect a connection with the New York line, that it lost out to the New Jersey Midland. Later reorganized as the New York & Greenwood Lake Railway, it reached only up near the state line to the south end of Greenwood Lake. The construction of the Wanaque Reservoir in the 1950's precipitated the abandonment of much of the line and today it extends only a mile or so past the Pompton Junction crossing.

ABOVE RIGHT: The "Butler Day Express" crosses the Pequannock River just west of Pompton Junction. Train 915 operated only four days a year: Election Day, Good Friday, Christmas and New Year's eves. Leaving Susquehanna Transfer at 1:30 PM, it was run for the convenience of people who got off work early on the holidays. It became a local institution with the railfans because it afforded one of the few chances at getting good photos of a train on the west end. The fans furnished a tailsign for the train, cleaned the windows, added Christmas decorations each year, and even got authority from the railroad to produce a special timetable for the Express' runs.

LEFT: An immaculate G-15a Ten-wheeler, the 970, heads for Butler with a train of Stillwells in February of 1941. In the distance is the bridge over the Pequannock seen in the previous photo, and the signal near the end of the train is the eastbound approach signal for Pompton Junction. The Bloomingdale passing track in the foreground also had a spur running off of it to serve sand and gravel banks. The Bloomingdale station lies ahead a short distance, and even in the early 1940's only a handful of trains stopped there. By the early 1950's, it was no longer a timetable stop.

JOHN L. TREEN

JOHN L. TREEN

VINCENT EMMANUEL

Butler

Butler, as the westernmost end of the commuter zone, was an important terminal and boasted a modest engine servicing facility and yard. ABOVE LEFT: The last steam operation on the Susquehanna is seen here as leased Erie K-1 Pacific No. 2530 takes water just west of the station prior to taking Train 924 east to Jersey City. The date is October 29, 1947 and for a six week period in late September and October, the NYS&W leased Erie steam power while their own diesels underwent their first major repairs. Additional orders for diesel locomotives received that month would preclude the necessity of ever using steam again and it seemed fitting that the redoubtable K-1's should perform the final steam runs. ABOVE RIGHT: A close up of the large, rambling Butler station now the Butler Museum. In the background can be seen the plant of the Pequannock Soft Rubber Company. The plant was destroyed in a spectacular inferno in February of 1957 that saw the Susquehanna men successfully pull locomotives and coaches to safety at their own peril. East of the station stood the American Hard Rubber Company, whose principal business was lining tank cars that carried corrosive chemicals.

BELOW LEFT: MC 1005-1006 at Butler on November 17, 1947, on a trial run eastbound before beginning regular service on the twentieth. The Susquehanna bought their first two Streamliners, 1001 and 1002, in June 1940 fresh from the factory of American Car & Foundry. The streamliners were sold to a number of other roads and in December of 1940, ACF delivered two cars to the Illinois Central. Car No. 130 was named the *Illini* and ran between Chicago and Champaign, while No. 131 was named *Miss Lou* for the two states it traversed on its run from Jackson, Miss. to New Orleans. The *Miss Lou* was apparently something of a success, but the *Illini's* schedule was pulled from the tables in the fall of 1941 and the car was renumbered 142 and renamed *Land O' Corn*. Just previous to this, IC had purchased a two-car Streamliner set, Nos. 140 and 141, named *Land O' Corn* also, to provide service from Chicago to Waterloo, Iowa. Apparently the old *Illini* car was pulled to serve as protect power for the *Land O' Corn* and the *Illini* schedule was reinstated with a locomotive hauled train. After all this work, the Illinois Central remained dissatisfied with the cars and returned all four of them to the builder in late 1942 or early 1943. ACF took the *Illini* and the *Miss Lou*, one of which had been severly damaged in a grade crossing accident, and rebuilt both cars into a semi-permanently coupled two car Streamliner set which went to the Susquehanna in the summer of 1943. Unfortunately, the trade journals of the period give the mistaken impression that the new Susquehanna cars, MC 1003 and 1004, were entirely brand new rather than being the ex-IC rebuilt cars that they really were. As best can be determined, the two original *Land O' Corn* units simply gathered dust at the ACF plant for more than four years before the Susquehanna finally purchased them in November 1947. By the fall of 1950, the Susquehanna had used the surviving streamliners as trade in material on the new Budd cars. Despite occasional rumors that the streamliners were sold to Cuba, the Budd Company records show that only a small amount of airbrake equipment was salvaged from the cars and that the bodies were cut up at North Hawthorne.

RIGHT: The 248 and the 250 grind their way past the storefronts of Butler on the way west to Hainesburg. Ahead the grade will become much stiffer as the track snakes and climbs up the valley of the Pequannock River.

BELOW RIGHT: The date is July 5, 1952 and Budd car M-2 stands ready at Butler station to head east to the Transfer. The gleaming railcar is only a little more than two years old, having been purchased in May of 1950. The demos had originally been numbered 2996 and 2997, but became M-1 and M-2; M-3 and M-4 joined them in October of 1950. Only eight years later, in April of 1958, the failing road sold the RDC1's to the Central Railroad of New Jersey. They have continued to run on the CNJ right through the Conrail era.

BELOW: Two examples of the Susquehanna's modest car fleet relegated to company service at Butler. The Susquehanna never had a particularly large car fleet and as might be expected, they were all Erie designs. One of the more unusual types was a large group of over 400 coal hoppers which discharged their load out to the side rather than between the rails. In this photo the hopper is a 50 ton steel car of the USRA design formulated during World War I. The boxcar is a somewhat older car, and the two are fairly typical of what was left when the Susquehanna went off on its own. It's somewhat curious that the road bought so much passenger equipment, but it's only purchase of interchange cars was the order for 35 standard PS-1 boxcars delivered by Pullman-Standard in November of 1952. The cars were later adorned with the Susie Q herald; a short lived and never popular herald showing a girl railroader (Susie Q) holding up a lantern to show the way. The cars became a victim of the great equipment sell-off. In the early 1960's, 33 of the original 35 cars were sold to the Monon Railroad and the remaining two were held for company service, leaving the Susquehanna with no interchange fleet.

JOHN L. TREEN

JOHN L. TREEN

JEFFREY K. WINSLOW

47

ABOVE LEFT: J-2 Russian No. 2435 leads the last mixed train from Sussex through the tiny hamlet of Excelsior Mills. Only a little more than a mile remains before tying up at Butler, and the failing light of a winter's day is casting long shadows over the little train. The mixed service on the Hanford branch came to an end on March 22, 1941, and was the final chapter on passenger service on the one time mainline that was to have been part of the great Midland Route. The line saw milk trains and expresses to Middletown, N.Y. through the early years of this century, but in the end it was only a baggage-mail combine car tied in with freight for the M&U connection at Hanford.

BELOW LEFT: A broader look at the Excellsior Mills that gave their name to the locale and furnished revenue to the railroad. The scenery west of Butler remains largely undisturbed today and looks much as it did in the 1940's. The track has been out of service since a washout at Smoke Rise cut the line in 1971, and today's visitor will be shocked at the substantial trees growing between the ties, and the fallen rock laying upon the rail.

ROBERT F. COLLINS

VINCENT EMMANUEL

ABOVE LEFT: An unusual view of a Jordan spreader at work, ditching along the main a mile or so east of old Green Pond Junction. Down below are the new lanes recently added to Route 23, which parallels most of the S&W main all the way up the valley to Stockholm.

ABOVE RIGHT: A closer look at the spreader, perhaps one of the most ingenious pieces of rail equipment to be seen. It may come as a surprise, given the demise of so many of the old time rail equipment builders, to know that the O.F. Jordan Company is still securely in business, continuing to produce the unique machines they introduced in 1900.

RIGHT: The Susquehanna's Jordan spreader, numbered 0279, was not a new machine, as evidenced by this photo taken in November of 1948, showing ex-Lehigh Valley 96769 shortly after purchase by the S&W and before being repainted and outfitted for service.

Perhaps the most interesting part of

this story is not shown by the photos at all. The date is August 17, 1955 and that night the East coast was struck by the first warning rains of hurricane Diane, which inflicted more damage over a wider area than perhaps any other storm of this century. The Delaware River ran nearly 30 feet above normal, and the damage to the railroads in New Jersey and Pennsylvania was incredible. What had started out as a simple ditching job proved to be a long stretch out on the road, as the spreader was pressed into service to assist in repairing the flood damaged main line. It was to be a week before the mainline to Hainesburg was reopened and more than two weeks before the Hanford branch could be repaired. It seems ironic that the flood hit just prior to the severe recession that caused the Susquehanna so much grief, for it was almost 20 years earlier that the '36 floods had hit the railroad so hard, only a year before they were plunged into bankruptcy.

ABOVE LEFT: An imminent collision? No, not at all; Eng. 250 pulls up to the rear of a Hainesburg freight which has stopped to drop cars for the Jersey Central at old Green Pond Junction. The locomotive ahead is the pusher engine assigned to assist the freight up the mountain to Beaver Lake. The tough grades on the Susquehanna often required pusher engines well through the diesel era. The pushers would often leave Little Ferry with a train and stay on right through to Hainesburg, for the return trip back up Sparta mountain was no easier than the westbound run. The date is June 3, 1949 and the frequency and length of the trains both indicate the Susquehanna's relative prosperity.

ABOVE RIGHT: Jim Boyd caught the 1800 on the new bridge just below old Green Pond Junction not long before the 1971 washout at Smoke Rise put an end to service west of Butler. The line to Sparta had already been embargoed and the Jersey Central connection was as far west as the GP18 would go. The substantial looking bridge had been installed in the fall of 1958 when the Charlotteburg Reservoir was built and the outlet was routed under the Susquehanna track just below the old CNJ connection at Green Pond Junction. The structure was entirely paid for by the City of Newark and in the background can be seen the chlorination plant. A switch was installed just east of the bridge and the Susquehanna did a steady business for some time delivering tank cars of chlorine to the plant.

RIGHT: A drab January day in 1949, and the 242 and 244 are safely in the hole at old Green Pond Junction, coupled to their delivery from the Jersey Central and waiting to head east. First they will have to back up and clear the yard tracks on the right to allow the Hainesburg extra coming up the hill to pull in and make their drop of cars for the CNJ.

ABOVE LEFT: The sunlight filtering through the trees at old Green Pond Junction plays shadows over the distinctive baby face of a CNJ Baldwin set. The DR 4-4-15 models are only about a year old in this November 1948 scene. The Central bought ten of the units and five companion B-units; in an unusual practice, the B-units were given letters only and the A-units, numbers. The front number boards had removable characters and when a lashup was made, the boards would be set up to reflect the units, for on the CNJ the entire lashup was considered to be one locomotive. Thus 77L79 is units 77 and 79 spliced by B-unit "L".

ABOVE RIGHT: A quick turnaround and brakeman Treen recorded the Baldwins pulling their delivery into the yard. An M&U job occupies one track and two more are filled with cars, leaving no free track for a runaround. Thus the Hainesburg job, whose units can be seen on the S&W main at the right, has pulled up clear of the junction switch and let the CNJ out on the Susquehanna main to grab the cars, rather than deliver them on the yard tracks as would be the more common practice.

RIGHT: On September 16, 1951, the CNJ delivery at old Green Pond included a rare sight: the first five of 16 new stainless steel coaches being delivered by the Budd Company of Philadelphia.

BELOW: A better look at the 85-foot coaches. Budd introduced the concept of stainless steel as a structural material rather than just a decorative extra during the 1930's. Most of their early cars were custom built for specific name trains, but by the war's end they had a standardized 85-foot body with which they produced coaches, diners, sleepers, lightweight commuter cars, and even the RDC's, which were nothing more than a beefed-up coach with a power system added. Although the ACF streamliners had been air conditioned, the Susquehanna declined the a/c option on their coaches. When the bottom fell out of the commuter service, the railroad tried to recover some of their investment and sold all 16 coaches in 1961 to the Saudi Arabian Government Railways, where reportedly they are still running. They were replaced by six ex-Delaware & Hudson, ex-Boston & Albany coaches.

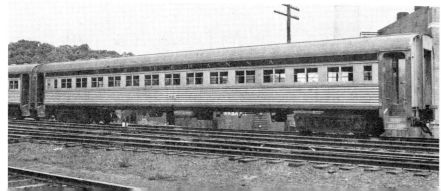

ROBERT F. COLLINS

RIGHT: A pair of GP18's skirts the massive retaining wall of the Charlotteburg Reservoir, heading east with a train from new Green Pond Junction. The year is 1962, and the previous year saw the abandonment of the Lehigh & New England and the cutback of the Susquehanna to Sparta Junction. The Charlotteburg Reservoir, constructed during 1958 and 1959, was formed by damming the Pequannock River to furnish water for the City of Newark. The reservoir flooded parts of the Jersey Central's Wharton & Northern line and forced the City to relocate the W&N track to a point west of old Green Pond Junction. In this view, the CNJ tracks are just visible to the left, swinging around the edge of the water to a connection with the Susquehanna. Today, the old Green Pond Junction is virtually impossible to locate. The lead engine is just about to hit the frog of the east switch of Macopin siding. The 25 car siding once led off to the right up a mile and half spur to Macopin Lake, more often called Echo Lake. The Macopin Lake Railroad was chartered in 1886 and opened for business in May of 1887. For many years a thriving excursion business was carried on to the lake. In 1900, the City of Newark purchased the lake for a water supply and refused to allow the excursions any longer. More durable was the ice harvesting business, which saw as many as 20,000 tons of ice a year taken from the lake. The old-timers on the Susquehanna tell some hair raising stories about bringing ice trains down the spur. Reportedly, an ice train would not be allowed to leave the Macopin Lake station until the dispatcher had cleared the main of all trains. Coming down the hill with both air brakes and handbrakes set, the trains would often tear right through Macopin siding and on down the main before finally coming to a halt. The ice business finally declined when mechanical refrigeration became common in the 1920's. The branch was torn up and the first relocation of Route 23 in the mid-1930's virtually obliterated all traces of the once-thriving branch.

JOHN L. TREEN

ABOVE: An extremely rare view of a G-15a Ten-wheeler, No. 969, heading upgrade near Charlotteburg with a wartime Beaver Lake train on August 8, 1943. In response to the imposition of wartime gas rationing in 1942, the Susquehanna extended service from Butler to Beaver Lake. The trains were put on in the fall of 1942, ran through 1943, but were lopped off in the spring of '44 when revenues failed to meet expenses. Understandably, there were severe restrictions on photographing trains during the war, and it was an extremely lucky circumstance that Bob Collins was able to catch the handsome Erie 4-6-0 and its train of Stillwells during the short and trying period when they worked west of Butler.

RIGHT: A pair of RS1's head back down the main to old Green Pond Junction after dropping their train in the clear at Macopin (Mock-a-pin) siding. Often a westbound would leave the train at Macopin and go down and clear up at old Green Pond for a meet with a train coming down the mountain. Eastbound trains coming down the hill were also required to stop and set up retainers at Macopin. In practice, they would often do the set-up while delivering cars at old Green Pond, and on short trains, the retainers would be dispensed with, especially after AB brakes became common.

ABOVE LEFT: From his crow's nest perch atop an RS1, John Treen photographed new Green Pond Junction in March 1959, shortly after the new interchange was opened for service. According to the timetables, it was officially known as W&N Junction (for the CNJ's Wharton & Northern line), but the old names die hard and it was most often referred to as "new" Green Pond. This view looks east on the Susquehanna down the hill and the track at the right was used for delivering cars to the CNJ.

ABOVE RIGHT: Looking west along the substantial length of the CNJ delivery, the S&W main lies to the right; to the left is the wye track used to turn the CNJ locomotives. The substantially built tracks belie the financial condition of both the Susquehanna and the Jersey Central, for all of this track is new construction paid for by the City of Newark. The Wharton & Northern line was carried in the *Official Guide* under its own name rather than under the CNJ listing, extending 15 miles from the end of the High Bridge branch at Lake Junction. It was the northernmost extension of the CNJ in New Jersey. **RIGHT:** Four years later, in the early spring of 1963, the GP18's have displaced the RS1's on the Susquehanna. The "baby-face" Baldwins of the CNJ, wearing a new paint scheme, continue to deliver cars at new Green Pond.

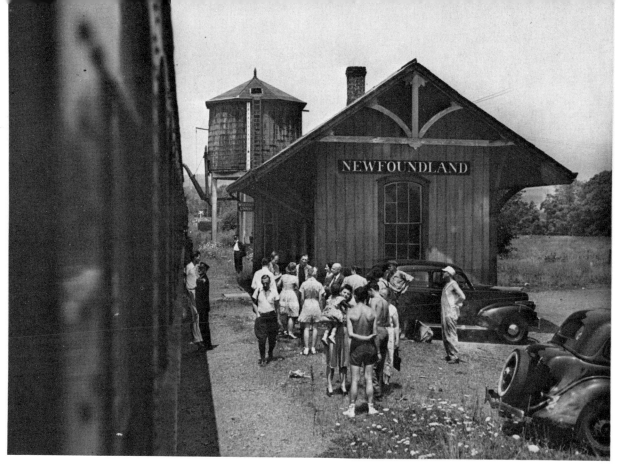

RAILFAN: JIM BOYD   VINCENT EMMANUEL

ABOVE: When we first began to research the Susquehanna, we learned of the wartime Beaver Lake service and frankly doubted that a photo of these trains could be uncovered. Imagine our surprise when not one (P. 52), but two photos from two different lensmen surfaced. In this classic meeting the train shot, we see the Newfoundland station in the summer of 1943.

RIGHT: More than twenty-five years later, the Newfoundland station is showing its age, but still looks surprisingly neat as a two car train from Green Pond drifts down the hill. The station has been leased to a fuel oil dealer, who has given the building a fresh coat of paint.

JOHN KRAUSE

 JOHN KRAUSE

ABOVE LEFT: After the 1971 washout at Smoke Rise, it seemed as though this portion of the Susquehanna would never see a train again, much less steam powered passenger trains. But on July 4, 1974, a crowd was on hand at the Newfoundland station for the opening of the Morris County Central operation. The MCC was the creation of Earl Gil and had first begun operation in 1965 on the tracks on the shortline Morristown & Erie at Whippany, N.J. After nine successful years on the M&E, it was decided to find a more scenic location and a lease was secured on the unused NYS&W track from Newfoundland to Beaver Lake. The equipment was moved from the M&E over a roundabout route that brought it to Sparta Junction on the Lehigh & Hudson River, where the old interchange track to the S&W was temporarily replaced to get the equipment on to Susquehanna rails. The MCC established an enginehouse at Newfoundland, which seemed fitting, for the old New Jersey Midland had once maintained engine facilities there when they first opened their line from Hackensack to Newfoundland in March of 1872.

BELOW LEFT: The doubleheaded locomotives between Newfoundland and Oak Ridge on a Fall Foliage Special. An anonymous shopman applied the neatly-lettered Susquehanna banner to the tender for the day and there were few, if any, who faulted the idea. The lead engine, No. 385, is an ex-Southern 2-8-0, a Baldwin graduate of 1907 that served its later years on the Virginia Blue Ridge shortline. The 4039 also came from the VBR, a fairly modern (1942) Alco 0-6-0 originally constructed for the U.S. Army.

ABOVE CENTER: It has been said that today's tourist railroads best recreate the mixed train, shortline era of the 1920's. A favorable comparison can be seen in this view of Train 930, the last eastbound mixed train from Sussex, descending the valley of the Pequannock

ROBERT F. COLLINS

C. GEORGE KRUMM

JOHN KRAUSE

on the afternoon of March 22, 1941. The mixed is riding the fill above the Oak Ridge Reservoir, another ward of the City of Newark, and the second lanes of Route 23 have yet to encroach upon the fill. Oak Ridge station lies about a half-mile ahead of the mixed and was moved off the property in 1942 to become a fuel oil dealer's office.

ABOVE RIGHT: We thought it would be interesting to see how two photographers approach the same subject. Bob Collins and George Krumm, both warned of the final run of the mixed, beat out of work early and headed for Sussex to chase the last run of the train. Stopping along Route 23, Bob scurried up the bank for a head-on shot with scenery; while in this photo, George opted for more of a broadside that showed the equipment. Russian Decapod No. 2435 seems like an awful lot of power for the Stillwell combine and the short train of freight cars. The combine was built by American Car & Foundry in 1934, part of an order for six combination cars and the last 50 Stillwell coaches to be ordered. The Erie apparently purchased them to protect both the parcel business and the mail contracts on those lines where mixed trains were being substituted for regular passenger trains. After the demise of the Hanford mixed, the 639 worked the Butler commuter runs until February of 1956, when it was sold to the Industrios y Commercio de Mineros railroad in Brazil.

BELOW RIGHT: Thirty-three years later, coal smoke drifts through the valley of the Pequannock once again as the inaugural run of the Morris County Central crosses the river nearing Stockholm. The concrete pier in the center of the bridge was added in the early 1920's to allow the Russians to work west of Butler. Just ahead is the site of the Stockholm station, torn down years before, where the run around is made for the return trip of the MCC trains.

ABOVE LEFT: A Russian 2-10-0 almost at the summit between Stockholm and Beaver Lake in September of 1940. The 2475 has been away at the O&W shops in Middletown and has returned, rebuilt and lettered Susquehanna. The long coal drag is bound for Hanford and a connection with the Middletown & Unionville where the M&U will convey the cars back to the O&W for loading on the Ontario's Scranton Division. Right through to the end of World War II, a substantial coal business was carried on from the O&W via the M&U, a shadow of what had once rolled off the Susquehanna's own Wilkes-Barre & Eastern extension to the coal fields.

ABOVE: An undated view from the same period of a G-class Ten-wheeler, still lettered for the Erie, rolling west through Beaver Lake yards with the mixed train for Sussex. The actual summit of the grade lies east of Beaver Lake, and more than one engineer ended up stalled at Beaver Lake when he was deceived into shutting off too soon. **LEFT:** The severe winter of 1947-48 brought an unusual visitor to the Beaver Lake yard in the form of a wooden Russell snow plow, leased from the Jersey Central to clear the Hanford Branch. Engine 250 is about to enter the branch track to begin plowing; near Quarryville, almost to the state line, they found cuts filled with ten and twelve feet of snow and the old wooden plow proved its mettle once again as the crew repeatedly punched at the drifts before finally breaking through.

Beaver Lake to Hanford

LEFT: An overview of Beaver Lake yard in the early spring of 1949. The 238 lies in the clear at the right with the steam crane in tow, while at the left, the 250 picks up cars off the Hanford Branch yard track. It's quite evident that the yard once contained much more trackage and as the 1940 era photo on the previous page shows, it has been out for a long time. There is no trace, however, of the enginehouse and company boarding house which once stood in the forested area to the right in the days when Beaver Lake was a division point on the Susquehanna. When the old New Jersey Midland first built here, the area between Stockholm and Beaver Lake was still known as Snufftown. A number of snuff mills were located in the area, dating from the era when every self respecting gentleman carried a tin of the powdered tobacco compound. When the Wilkes-Barre & Eastern extension was opened in 1882, Two Bridges, as the station was known, became the division point for trains running to Gravel Place, and by 1894 all the way to Wilkes-Barre. Sometime around the turn of the century, the station acquired its present name of Beaver Lake. The station saw passenger trains bound for Stroudsburg and Wilkes-Barre on the main line, and Middletown via the Hanford Branch, milk trains, and most of all the coal trains. The crews who worked west to Pennsylvania were a boisterous and hardy bunch known simply as the mountain men. The anthracite decline in the 1920's put an end to Beaver Lake's glory days and today's generation finds it hard to believe that this was once a bustling division point.

ABOVE: A view looking east around the curve towards the Beaver Lake station, nestled in the shadow of the Route 23 highway bridge. A Hainesburg extra is shoving back into Track 1 to pick up empties bound for the LNE connection. The station and the handcar shed are all that is left at Beaver Lake in this late-1940's photo. At the lower left, just out of sight, there once stood a 200-foot long ice house which held ice for the refrigerator cars on the milk trains.

ABOVE: A closer look at the Beaver Lake station from the Route 23 highway bridge. The building remains one of the very few stations west of Butler that has survived the abandonments and service cutbacks. The Morris County Central lease extends to Beaver Lake, and although trips normally tie up near Stockholm, an occasional special will run all the way to Beaver Lake.

ABOVE RIGHT: A scene from the top of the caboose as the 230 and 238 grind their way eastbound up to Beaver Lake station in April 1958. The station is just out of sight around the curve. The track to the left is the Hanford Branch, which parallels the main for some distance west of Beaver Lake at a lower level. The open area to the right was once the site of the wye track which replaced a turntable near the station sometime before World War I.

RIGHT: In the spring of 1951, the old wye track was yet to be taken up. The track off the east leg in the foreground is the survivor of two team tracks which went back to the days when a team of horses would carry off the unloaded freight. Perhaps a thousand feet or so around the curve in the distance stood the coal pocket and water tank. Taking advantage of gravity, the water tank was fed by a pipe from the creek at the wye track. The coal pocket was also located on the Hanford Branch track and was fed by gravity from the main. This meant that a mainline train needing coal and water would have to stop on the main, cut the engine and run up past a set of crossovers just east of the wye track and then back down the Hanford Branch to get coal and water. Hurricane Diane in 1955 caused a massive washout at the site of the old coal pocket and water tank and obliterated all traces of the structures.

Because the line splits at Beaver Lake, we shall first follow the Hanford Branch before continuing our traverse of the mainline. West of Beaver Lake, the main and the branch paralleled each other for about two and a half miles as the branch continued to drop down towards Ogdensburg. Within ¾ miles of the Ogdensburg station there stood a small hard coal storage facility similar to the larger storage piles at Coalberg Yard. The facility was accessible only from the Hanford Branch side and was abandoned before World War I.

ABOVE LEFT: We've often seen photos of old boxcars or coaches set on the ground for use as structures, so we were rather intrigued by this view of the carpenter gang setting off an old boxcar at Ogdensburg in September 1949 for use as a freight house. The old freight house and passenger station were directly across the tracks out of sight to the right. Much of the trackage east and west of the Ogdensburg station rests on a moraine left by the last ice age. The huge deposit of glacial rock and dirt formed a natural fill for the builders of the Midland and explains why the Hanford Branch could cut so sharply across the valley of the Walkill River in comparison to the main line.

BELOW LEFT: Just across the short manmade fill from Ogdensburg station stood the New Jersey Zinc Company plant and in this November 1948 view, the 234 is pulling six cars out of the plant: empty coal hoppers from the power plant and loaded ore cars of the Lehigh & Hudson River Railway. The zinc ore was carried to the L&HR connection at Franklin Junction to be forwarded to the smelter at Palmerton, Pa. The Hanford Branch crew has left their train up on the mainline fill and gone down in the "hole" to get the cars out of the plant. The grade into the zinc company is so steep that six cars is about all an RS1 could drag out of there. The Ogdensburg operation, although not as old as the Franklin mines, dated back to the early years of this century. When Franklin mine was played out and closed in September 1954, Ogdensburg became the sole facility in the area. Coincidentally with abandonment of the Hanford Branch in 1958, a combination of depressed prices caused by Canadian competition and a protracted strike caused the Ogdensburg mine to be shut down for more than a year. When it finally reopened, an arrangement was made to sell the track from Franklin Junction to the mine to the Lehigh & Hudson, who then took over servicing the plant.

BELOW: A good look at the plant trackage and the loading bins as a pair of L&HR Century 420's switch the zinc company in 1974. The overhead conveyor leads off to the shafts on the hillside out of sight to the right. The ore is only crushed at Ogdensburg and the smelting is done at the central facility at Palmerton. In April 1976, the L&HR became one of the components of Conrail, and the zinc company is perhaps the principal reason that Conrail continues to operate the L&HR trackage.

ABOVE LEFT: A Hanford bound freight drops slowly down into Franklin in the fall of 1948. Just barely discernible in the distance is the roof of the Franklin station. The first railroad to reach Franklin was neither the L&HR nor the Susquehanna, but the old Sussex Railroad of New Jersey. In 1870, the Sussex Railroad built a line from Branchville Junction, near Newton, to Franklin Furnace. An iron furnace was in operation at Franklin, and although zinc was being mined, it would be quite a few years before the zinc industry would overshadow the iron industry. The Sussex Railroad dated to 1849 and eventually became part of the Lackawanna in 1881. The Sussex got to Franklin just as the New Jersey Midland was building west and rather than build their own station, it was more expedient for the NJM to purchase a half equity in the existing (and brand new) Sussex Railroad station. Franklin Furnace became simply Franklin in 1926 and in 1936, the Lackawanna abandoned the branch and sold their share of the station and the associated trackage to the Susquehanna. The building came down just a few years before the entire Hanford Branch was abandoned.

BELOW LEFT: The Lehigh & Hudson River station at Franklin Junction in 1954. Although Franklin and Franklin Junction were only about a half mile apart, Susquehanna trains stopped at both the joint S&W-DL&W station and also at the L&HR station.

ABOVE RIGHT: The diamond at Franklin Junction in November 1948 looking west on the Susquehanna towards Hanford and east on the L&HR to Warwick. To the right is the huge complex of the New Jersey Zinc Company, being switched by L&HR No. 62, a camelback 2-8-0. The light track on the L&HR's Mine Hill Branch kept both 52 and 62 in service until the end of steam on the L&HR in 1950. The predecessors of New Jersey Zinc began mining at Franklin in 1848, long before any railroad arrived. Metallic zinc had been isolated as early as 1741, but from simple ore. The complex zinc-iron-manganese ore know as franklinite defied smelting until after the Civil War. In the interim, the zinc company found a way to make zinc oxide from the ore and established the first successful man made paint pigment. The incredibly rich deposits at Franklin, coupled with new smelting techniques, made the New Jersey Zinc Company grow by leaps and bounds. A separate drill job was assigned on the L&HR just to switch the plant. By the early 1950's, however, the ores were playing out and the only veins worth working were already penetrated by shafts from Ogdensburg, so the Franklin mine was closed in September 1954 and all mining transferred to Ogdensburg.

BELOW RIGHT: A companion view on the same day looking east on the S&W. The L&HR station is out of sight behind the company houses at the right. The crossing of both the DL&W and the Susquehanna were protected by interlocking signals. An L&HR train had only to stop at either diamond and when the signal cleared, it could pass over both diamonds. When the Franklin Branch of the DL&W was torn up in 1936, the signals were arranged to continue to provide interlocking for the remaining two roads. Because the L&HR arrived last, they were obligated to maintain the protection and thus the signals are L&HR upper quadrant semaphores.

C. GEORGE KRUMM

The mixed train to Sussex looks particularly impressive coming through Hamburg on January 11, 1941, just two months before the mixed was cut off. The Susquehanna tracks are curving around to parallel the Lehigh & Hudson up on the fill in the background. The L&H station was just out of sight behind the hill while the Susquehanna's Hamburg station was over on the other side of town. The reverse curves at Hamburg on the L&H were the site of more than one derailment that spilled cars down on to the S&W tracks. The mixed is just past the famed Gingerbread Castle opened in 1930 by businessman F.H. Bennett on the site of a former flour mill along the Walkill River. Bennett had hired Broadway set designer Joseph Urban to design a fairy tale castle that would illustrate the fabled stories of the Grimm Brothers and the castle continues to delight thousands of children yearly. Visitors are still admonished not to touch the gingerbread walls lest they turn to stone.

WILLIAM S. YOUNG   JOHN L. TREEN

ABOVE LEFT: The scrap train at work dismantling the Lehigh & New England just east of Sussex in May 1962. The camera looks west towards Hainesburg and the vacant piers in the foreground once carried the Susquehanna over the L&NE's Hainesburg-Maybrook (N.Y.) main line. The L&NE entered Sussex proper on a 0.7-mile spur known as the Deckertown Extension, which left the main west of this spot. Just behind the camera, an interchange track curved off of the L&NE and up the hill to connect with the S&W, but given the joint trackage between Swartswood and Hainesburg and the L&NE's own line into Sussex, the interchange was never used in later years although it remained in place until the Hanford Branch was torn up in 1958.

ABOVE RIGHT: The 234 has stopped in the clear east of Sussex station in the fall of 1949, and the head man is about to cut the engine off and pull down into the station yard to do some switching. Like so many other Susquehanna stations, Sussex had changed names since the road was first built and was once known as Deckertown.

RIGHT: The date is March 22, 1941 and Decapod No. 2435 pulls out of the Sussex yard and up to the station to pick up passengers for the last run of the mixed train. The mixed left Butler in the early morning hours and arrived at Sussex at 9:20 AM. The combine would be dropped at Sussex and the train would continue to the M&U connection at the state line. By 2:00 PM the engine was back in Sussex and ready to head east again. Right up until the last years, another freight only job worked the line to Hanford during the night hours.

HOWARD E. JOHNSTON PHOTO. COURTESY RAYMOND W. BROWN

ABOVE: The simple, yet handsome Sussex station in the fall of 1945 as a local switches the yard. Note that the Railway Express truck still finds occasion to call at the depot for l.c.l. freight and although the mixed has been gone for four years, the baggage cart is still put to good use in handling parcels. The Lehigh & New England maintained its own station in another part of town. It's amazing today to see some of the rural towns such as this that once boasted two and sometimes three separate rail depots in the heyday of rail travel. BELOW: A look at the Sussex yard looking east towards the station. Sussex is a farm center for this area of New Jersey and after losing the Susquehanna in 1958, the shippers got together in 1962 and organized their own company in a futile attempt to keep the LNE from also pulling out. They could not raise enough cash to purchase the LNE track from Sussex to the Lackawanna at Augusta and the town lost its second and last rail connection.

JOHN L. TREEN

JOHN L. TREEN

RIGHT: Decapod 2443 still wearing the Erie diamond, rolls through the open country east of Quarryville headed for Sussex. The date is March 31, 1940, and the Susquehanna has just completed its first month of independent operation. The 2-10-0 sports white extra flags in deference to the scheduled mixed train that still works the Hanford Branch. The Quarryville station once furnished large quantities of blue stone loadings from a quarry west of the station. The station disappeared in 1939, but the rock cuts in the area furnished wintertime headaches for as long as the branch was operated as they were notorious for filling with drifting snow.

BELOW LEFT: A view from the "gig-top" window of an M&U extra pulling into the junction at Hanford. As the open land will testify, Hanford was more of a locale than a thriving community of any kind, and merely happened to be where the Susquehanna finally hit the New York-New Jersey borderline. There was never a station here: the next stop was in Unionville, N.Y, and Hanford was only an artificial point created when the Susquehanna gave up its control of the M&U's predecessor in 1913 and stopped running into New York altogether.

BELOW RIGHT: The ten steel cabooses, numbered 0110 to 0119, arrived in the fall of 1948 from the International Car Company, a new postwar entry into the carbuilding field specializing in cabooses and whose standardized designs have come to dominate the industry. The new steel cabins replaced a group of older wooden Erie hacks that dated to the early years of the century.

ROBERT F. COLLINS

JOHN L. TREEN

JOHN L. TREEN

66

ABOVE: Middletown & New Jersey No. 1, a General Electric 44-tonner, pulls into Hanford in the fall of 1948. The black with white stripe paint scheme on the locomotive is a variation of a common GE painting diagram used for many of its customers, and is merely upside-down from that used on the Ontario & Western's 44-tonners.

BELOW: The Susquehanna's rudimentary facilities at Hanford: a single passing track and off to the left, an armstrong turntable. The view looks north and the state line is just around the curve in the distance. The original company, the Middletown Unionville & Water Gap railroad, was promoted by prominent Middletown businessmen to build south from their fair city to the Delaware Water Gap, the great natural break in the mountain walls along the Delaware River. The road was completed in 1868 only to the state line and was built to the Erie's six foot gauge, a common practice at the time when the Erie was encouraging the building of shortline feeders and leasing equipment to them to get them going. The line was leased by the Oswego Midland in 1871 to form the link between the Oswego Midland in New York and the New Jersey Midland and a third rail was laid to accomodate the standard gauge Midland trains. However, by 1873 the Oswego Midland was in bankruptcy and suspended lease payments to the MU&WG whereupon the New Jersey Midland stepped in and leased the property themselves. The lease was to be in perpetuity, yet in 1913 the Erie simply defaulted on the bond payments and let the lease go. That year was exceptionally prosperous and the Erie certainly had the money, so the question arises as to why they let the little road get away from them. Apparently the original lease had been quite generous in order to get the Water Gap away from the Oswego Midland. By 1913, any dreams of the old Midland route were long gone and there was no question that the Pennsylvania extension was the big money maker. It seems reasonable that the Erie could see no reason to keep making the payments, for they would surely get the traffic in any case, being the only connection on the south end of the line. The company reorganized as the Middletown & Unionville, dropping the Water Gap from its title. By 1946, the M&U was in serious financial trouble and was reorganized once again as the Middletown & New Jersey Railway, the name under which it continues to operate today.

JOHN L. TREEN

JOHN L. TREEN

The 232 idles at the Hanford interchange awaiting the arrival of the M&NJ on a beautiful summer's day in 1949. In their later years, the RS1's seemed to have constant problems with the radiator shutters functioning properly and the engine would overheat. To overcome this, the engine crew would simply leave enough side doors open to provide cooling. The Alco's, plowing through the weeds with the doors flapping back and forth, often looked like some monstrous tin bird moving over the land. When the Susquehanna gave up the lease of the MU&WG in 1913,

through service to Middletown discontinued. The S&W continued to run three trains a day to Hanford right up until the bankruptcy, roughly at morning, afternoon and evening intervals. After 1937, only a mixed ran as far as Sussex. Curiously enough, three separate westbounds to Hanford were run, but coming east again, the afternoon train would be combined at Beaver Lake with the eastbound mixed coming in from Stroudsburg to run to Jersey City as a single train.

RIGHT: M&U No. 7 pulls into the interchange at Hanford with a long string of Ontario & Western coal hoppers loaded with anthracite bound mostly for the factories of Paterson. The track at the right belongs to the M&U and the ungainly looking 2-8-0 is just about sitting on the state line. Coal traffic off the O&W still furnished considerable revenue to the Susquehanna through the end of the war when oil and gas finally killed off the hard coal business.

BELOW LEFT: The most frequent visitors to the Hanford interchange in the late 1930's and early 1940's were M&U No. 6 and 7. In this view, No. 6 reposes at Middletown. Originally built in 1908 for the O&W, the Cooke-built 4-4-0 was sold in 1935 to the M&U and was perhaps their handsomest piece of power.

BELOW RIGHT: Ungainly is perhaps the best description of No. 7, a lightweight 2-8-0 built in 1902 by Rhode Island for the predecessor of Henry Ford's Detroit Toledo & Ironton. As DT&I No. 76, the hog was sold off to a Pennsylvania shortline, the Bellefonte Central, where it served as their No. 16 before coming to the M&U in 1940. The war was not kind to either 6 or 7 and by 1944, they were both ready for the junkyard. To tide them over, the M&U leased two Russian decapods, the 2451 and 2461, from the Susquehanna. The tenders of the S&W 2-10-0's sported an unusual homemade lease plate stating that they were leased from the Susquehanna to the M&U. A bit of shortline ingenuity, the plates were cut with an oxyacetylene torch from sheet steel and were hand lettered with electric weld! When the M&U was reorganized in 1946 as the Middletown & New Jersey, the new company's first move was the purchase of a 44 ton GE diesel and the Decapods went back to the Susquehanna and the scrapyard.

ROBERT F. COLLINS

ROBERT F. COLLINS   ROBERT F. COLLINS

ABOVE: The northern terminus of the Middletown & Unionville was Middletown, N.Y., where it connected with the Erie and the Ontario & Western. Here were the NYO&W's main locomotive and car shops. As mentioned, the Susquehanna had no equipment of their own and leased Erie equipment to get them underway after March 1, 1940. The locomotives and cars were sent to Middletown to be repaired and painted by the O&W, for the Susquehanna had no shop facilities either, having all been closed down in the late 1920's in favor of the Erie shops. At this time, noted railroad historian and traction expert Steve Maguire was employed in the freight claims department of the O&W and was in a position to record the rebuilding of the Susquehanna's equipment. In this photo, Russian 2-10-0 No. 2452 lies waiting out behind the backshop at Middletown in the company of a torn down O&W Bullmoose 2-10-2 boiler loaded on a flat car. More photos and history of the NYO&W appear in the Carstens Publications book "The Final Years".

BELOW: The same 2452 is now being switched out for a trip through the shop by a V-class Camelback 2-6-0 No. 272. Unlike the Susquehanna center cabbers, the O&W Camelbacks saw active service right through to the end of steam on the road.

ABOVE: A sister 2-10-0, the 2495 stands polished and ready at the East Main Street station of the M&U for the return trip to the Susquehanna. The rebuildings were done under the supervision of Otto C. Gruenberg, the O&W's motive power super, who would return from the war to the Susquehanna rather than the O&W in the same role and eventually rise to become general manager of the S&W. The East Main Street station was the first terminus of the New Jersey Midland's through trains, but were extended later to tie up at the O&W's Wickham Avenue station.

BELOW: From the second floor window of the Wickham Avenue station, Steve Maguire also caught a brace of freshly repaired and painted Stillwell coaches being pulled down to the M&U interchange by a W class Consolidation. A center section of the station was a late 1930's addition to the building prompted by the economy of getting the office force out of the high rent offices in New York, and moving them to Middletown. However, part of the force was left in cheaper quarters on West 42nd Street in New York and they initially handled the Susquehanna's car accounting after the breakaway from the Erie. This work was moved to Middletown shortly afterwards and remained there until the Susquehanna opened their own offices in July 1942 in a commercial building opposite both the Susquehanna's Paterson City station and the Erie Paterson station. The Susquehanna hired a number of the O&W employees to work for them, and each morning a group of former O&W people would gather at the Erie's Middletown station for the ride to Paterson.

STEPHEN D. MAGUIRE

STEPHEN D. MAGUIRE

Beaver Lake West

ABOVE LEFT: We return to Beaver Lake to follow the Susquehanna main westward. In this 1962 view the station is beginning to look pretty bad, having been altered to house the motor cars and boarded up with an old crossbuck on one window.

BELOW LEFT: Maintenance was better in 1949 when the 238 took the steam crane west to pick up loose rocks that the spring thaw had dropped along the main. The crane is working partway down Sparta Mountain at a point where the track is running the ridge of the mountain to descend into Sparta.

BELOW: An eastbound train from Hainesburg swings around the broad curve east of Sparta station heading up the mountain to Beaver Lake. It is 1960 and in little more than a year, the Lehigh & New England will become a memory and the L&HR connection at Sparta Junction will become the westernmost end of the railroad.

JOHN KRAUSE   JOHN L. TREEN   JOHN KRAUSE

RIGHT: The 1800 heads west over the same bridge nearing Sparta station in 1962. It was this structure which the railroad declared to be unsafe when they embargoed the L&HR connection in 1969. Although it's certainly not the Rockville bridge or Starrucca viaduct, there was good reason to question the railroad's condemnation of the bridge. The embargoed cars were routed over the L&HR and the Erie to Passaic Junction for final delivery by the Susquehanna. This meant that the S&W got the delivering road charges and lost only a small part of the line haul money.

BELOW LEFT: Sparta station in the last years of service. Leased to a manufacturing concern for office space, the building has been well-preserved and is one of the very few stations still standing west of Beaver Lake. When the station was leased, the company constructed a small wooden water tank on the old standard Erie poured concrete foundation. The company manufactures industrial chemicals, and the processes require large volumes of water, thus the new tank on the old footings.

BELOW RIGHT; A quintet of RS1's pauses at the Sparta tank to take water in 1958 before heading up the mountain. Diesels, taking water?...we've mentioned the problems of overheating on the Alco road switchers and in this case, the second unit overheated so severely that it blew all its radiator water. The chemical company helped the engine crew hook up a temporary hose to the tank to refill the radiators. Sadly, as the railroad declined, each trip over the road became a new adventure for the beleagured Susquehanna crewmen as they contended with repeated engine failures and derailments.

JOHN KRAUSE

HAROLD H. CARSTENS

JOHN L. TREEN

73

N.Y.S.& W.
RAILROAD PROPERTY
NO TRESPASSING

JOHN KRAUSE

74

LEFT: GP18's Nos. 1804 and 1802 approach Sparta Junction from the east with a short train of cars for the L&HR in the spring of 1963. The shining EMD's, purchased with a Federal loan guarantee, tend to belie the declining fortunes of the road.

ABOVE RIGHT: A J-2 Russian, the 2475, pulls across the Lehigh & Hudson River diamond with a long train of wartime freight from Hainesburg. Note the Susquehanna freight house still standing at the left and the order board on the right for the L&H main. Although the Sparta Junction op's job belonged to the Susquehanna, they would occasionally write an order for an L&H train. The track curving off to the left is the interchange track that was reinstalled in 1973 to allow the Morris County Central equipment to get over to Susquehanna rails.

BELOW RIGHT: By June 1947, the Decapods and the freight house were gone as the 238 and 242 prepare to cross the L&H on their way to Hainesburg. The diamond was protected by a tilting board signal that was normally kept at the horizontal, indicating "Stop" for the Susquehanna. The S&W was required to stop and call the L&H dispatcher, who would give them permission to cross. After tilting the board to a 45° angle, the home signals on the L&H would go red and the Susquehanna was free to cross.

VINCENT EMMANUEL

JOHN L. TREEN

JOHN L. TREEN

JOHN L. TREEN

LEFT: The tilt board stands horizontal, holding the Susquehanna against the passage of an eastbound L&HR train. The RS1's of the Susquehanna seemed to be in good company with the RS3's of the L&HR and the FA's of the Lehigh & New England. At one point in the late 1950's, a rather exhaustive study was made of the possibility of abandoning the LNE's Maybrook line in favor of operating rights over the L&HR. It's interesting to conjecture what effect the move could have had on the eventual fortunes of all three companies.

ABOVE LEFT: Like the little Whitcombs that worked the Edgewater yard, the Susquehanna also had a miniature version of the Streamliners. MC 100 was purchased in 1940, right after independence, from the Buda Company, a manufacturer of small rail service cars and various shop machinery. In this April 1950 view the little inspection car is standing on the north leg of the wye, which leads off to the interchange track with the L&HR in the background. The little car was sold in the early 1960's to Liberia.

ABOVE RIGHT: Sperry Rail Service Car 118 lies on the south leg of the wye in November 1948, tied up for the weekend before going to work using their induction test devices on the Susquehanna rails. The Sperry principle employed a magnetic field which was induced in the rails. A defective rail would disturb the field and register on a recording device in the car. Sperry personnel were probably the most well read folks in the country, and perhaps the world's greatest card players, for the cars were notorious for tying up in the middle of nowhere, far removed from any form of entertainment. The legs of the Sparta Junction wye were diagonally opposite each other across the diamond.

RIGHT: The second 233 moves east across the diamond in 1949, running light back to Butler after assisting a train west to Hainesburg. The LNE won't be delivering enough cars today to require a pusher on the eastbound run, so 233 is going back light. The Susquehanna got amazing utilization out of their fleet of RS1's, but

JOHN KRAUSE

often played nip and tuck in the process. It was not uncommon to send a job to Hainesburg during the night with a pusher and have the train return in the early morning hours. Grinding up Sparta mountain, they would finally make Beaver Lake and the pusher would cut off and run ahead down the other side like a bucket down a well, trying to make Butler in time to protect the first eastbound commuter runs.

JOHN KRAUSE

ABOVE: The 1800 and 1804 grab its two cars off the interchange track in this 1962 view of Sparta Junction that looks east on the L&H towards Maybrook. Very little has changed at the junction in the intervening years, but to the west the scrappers are pulling up NYS&W rails and soon the diamond will be gone.

RIGHT: The 246 and 252 drag a long Hainesburg job eastbound over the DL&W crossing at Hyper-Humus, bound for Sparta Junction. In the background is the Susquehanna's Hyper-Humus station. This area has a rather long and intricate history. All of the land in the area was once the Warbasse (War'-bus) family farm and a Post Office and small community sprang up here. In 1866, the Sussex Railroad built through here on the way to Branchville; in 1870, they added the Franklin Branch, which left the main a quarter mile south at Branchville Junction. By 1881, control of the Sussex Railroad rested with the Lackawanna Iron & Steel Company, who had an offer from the newly formed Lehigh & Hudson to buy the Sussex Railroad. The Delaware Lackawanna & Western, alarmed at the prospect, quickly jumped in and bought the Sussex Railroad themselves. Coincidently, the Susquehanna was building west to Pennsylvania and crossings were installed at both the Franklin Branch and the Branchville line. At this point the reader should be cautioned: many old timetables and maps give the impression that Warbasse Junction, as the Susquehanna station was first known, is the same place as Branchville Junction on the DL&W. When the S&W was building, the natural contours of the land dictated that they parallel the Franklin Branch from a point just west of Sparta Junction over to Warbasse Junction. The first diamond crossing the Franklin Branch was roughly 3000 feet east of Warbasse Junction and was protected up through the 1920's by a signal tower. Between the two diamonds, a passing track extended nearly the whole length. Near the Warbasse Junction diamond the Lackawanna swings around in a quarter circle to hit the main Branchville line a quarter-mile south of the diamond and this point was Branchville Junction station on the DL&W. Warbasse Junction became simply Warbasse in later years and sometime in the mid-1930's was renamed to Hyper-Humus. The Franklin Branch was torn out in 1936, leaving only the diamond at Hyper-Humus. The tilting board signal protecting the diamond was identical in appearance to the one at Sparta Junction, but operated in a somewhat different manner. The Lackawanna was here first, so the Susquehanna was required to stop and clear the signal before crossing. There was no communication with the DL&W dispatcher; the crew relied simply upon a knowledge of the Lackawanna schedule and what could be seen coming. Like Sparta Junction, the normal position of the tilt board was horizontal for "Stop". When the signal was moved to the 45° position to clear the S&W, an unusual hookup of wire cables threw the DL&W semaphores to red.

BELOW: The 1121, a heavy Lackawanna 4-6-2, pulls a train of milk cars and coaches over the Hyper-Humus diamond in March of 1949. The train has come out of Branchville and is heading east for Newton and Netcong where they will hit the old main for the run to Hoboken. Directly ahead of the engine is a lower quadrant semaphore, but it is not for the diamond but rather an automatic block signal. If it seems to be in a strange location, it is because the Sussex Branch was signalled with a somewhat unusual two-signal system that essentially consisted of both a distant and home signal for each block in the manner of an interlocking. Visible along the track are the white posts supporting the sheave wheels that carry the cable down to the home signal for the diamond, out of sight to the right. The Hyper-Humus station is out of sight at the left. This curious signal arrangement disappeared a few years after this photo was taken and was replaced by a smash board on the Susquehanna that was interlocked electrically to the DL&W signals.

ROBERT F. COLLINS

JOHN L. TREEN

A view from the roof of the hack looking down the length of an eastbound approaching Hyper-Humus, with the engines almost even with the station. The LNE has delivered a respectable train on this fall day in 1950. By now, we're sure your curiosity has been whetted as to where the odd name of Hyper-Humus came from. The name dates to 1915, when the Hyper-Humus Company was formed to market the vast deposits of peat in the Warbasse area. The peat, known locally as "black dirt", occurs naturally in a number of places in northern New Jersey and parts of southern New York, but this deposit is by far the most extensive and also the richest. It has been worked continuously since 1915 and shows no sign of being depleted. The Susquehanna serviced the bagging plant from a switch west of the station. One of the great unknowns in local railfan circles was the existence of a two foot gauge railroad that crisscrossed the fields and brought the peat to the plant. It apparently dated to the beginnings of the operation and was operated with gasoline locomotives. None of the Hyper-Humus personnel know if steam locomotives were ever used. Peat has only half the density of topsoil and the narrow gauge continued to serve the plant well until the early 1950's, when trucks were finally introduced that were sufficiently large to economically handle the material. Incredibly, the equipment and rails lay at Hyper-Humus into the early 1970's before being sold off. The peat is used as a soil enricher for landscaping and gardens for the organic matter in the humus produces amazing results. The narrow gauge never physically connected with the Susquehanna, but only laced the fields and it's a shame that the operation remained so obscure and unrecorded over all the years that it ran.

Operator H.O. Brooks passes up the order to a westbound Lehigh & New England train at Swartswood Junction in April 1951. In the background, a Susquehanna work train lays in the clear on the S&W main. West of Hyper-Humus, the Susquehanna skirted the county seat of Newton through the small village of Halsey and dropped down into the valley of the Paulins Kills to Swartswood. During the construction of the line from Beaver Lake to Hainesburg in the early 1880's, the newly formed Susquehanna bought property and ran surveys for a branch into Newton, but it never materialized. The Lackawanna remained the only road in town. The track from Swartswood Junction to Hainesburg Junction belonged to the Susquehanna and was opened for business in 1882. Previous to this,

the predecessors of the LNE had surveyed and partly graded a parallel route, but they went through a whole maze of name changes, receiverships, and charter disputes that saw little progress made on actually building a line. The LNE was to have been a great trunk route from Philadelphia to Boston via the Poughkeepsie Bridge. It was opened in 1890 from Slatington, Pa. to Maybrook, N.Y. At that time, it was known as the Pennsylvania Poughkeepsie & Boston, and PP&B found it much more expedient to use the Susquehanna track from Hainesburg to Swartswood. The PP&B became the Lehigh & New England in 1895, and although they never gave up the title to their own right-of-way, it remained adequate throughout the life of the LNE to continue using Susquehanna trackage.

JOHN L. TREEN

JOHN L. TREEN

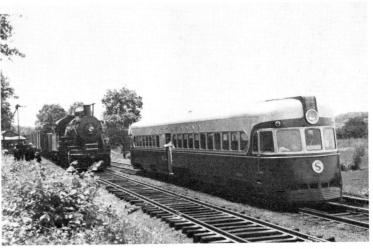

STEPHEN D. MAGUIRE

ABOVE: A rare view of one of the few occasions on which the streamliners ventured west of Butler. On June 23, 1940, the New York Division of the Railroad Enthusiasts chartered a trip on the Susquehanna, riding the freshly delivered streamliner 1001. Leaving Little Ferry, the trip was almost aborted by engine trouble, but a stop at North Hawthorne cured the railcar's ills and the special continued to Beaver lake and out the main. In this photo, the train is standing in the clear on the LNE main as a J-2 Russian Decapod passes eastbound by the operator's cabin at Swartswood Junction. A half mile further west was the actual Swartswood station, which survived until the end of service in 1962. The RRE excursion continued west all the way to Gravel Place, turned and returned to Beaver Lake for a side trip up the Hanford Branch. The streamliners were to venture west at least one more time. It's reliably reported that Walter Kidde organized at least one trip of the 1001 all the way to Gravel Place for the benefit of the officials and shippers of the road.

LEFT: The 252 and 248 passing Swartswood Junction; on the ground, operator Brooks holds the hoop with the orders for the rear end while engineer Butz tosses back the empty hoop after extracting his copy of the flimsies.

ROBERT F. COLLINS

On this page we present a trio of divergent photos all taken from the same location: the overhead highway bridge east of Stillwater station. They graphically illustrate the diversity of power that operated over the line.

ABOVE LEFT: The trees are bare and the sky overcast in this November 1942 scene, perhaps symbolic of the times as the nation agonizes through the first year of global war. The 2490, a Russian Decapod, has hold of only 16 cars as it heads up the valley of the Paulins Kill in the early morning light.

BELOW LEFT: The Standard Railroad of the World makes its presence felt in the rural hills of Sussex County as an ex-Pennsylvania Railroad L-1 Mikado lays down the smoke hauling 43 cars to Maybrook. The Lehigh & New England purchased four of the 2-8-2's during 1941 and they survived on the LNE until 1948, when the new Alco FA's sent them off to the dead line. Over on the other side of the mountain, the other "Lehigh" road, the Lehigh & Hudson River, rented L-1 Mikes regularly during the war from the PRR and it must have made an interesting sight to see the Pennsy steeds standing side by side in the Maybrook yard, far removed from their home rails.

BELOW: It's now April of 1957 and the terrain remains identical, but steam a fading memory. The time lapse is underscored by the fact that the first three RS1's wear the simplified maroon and gray paint scheme while the last unit has the economy silver paint job that appeared in 1955.

JOHN L. TREEN

ROBERT F. COLLINS

VINCENT EMMANUEL

JOHN KRAUSE

JOHN KRAUSE

RIGHT: The familiar Alco chant reverberates over the hills as a trio of RS1's head west past the Stillwater depot in 1960. The creamery behind the engines and the rolling hills beyond speak of the rural nature of this part of Sussex County and explain why the Susquehanna had little reason to keep this line intact after tenant Lehigh & New England was gone.

Researching a given railroad to any degree might well be termed "ulcers and euphoria"; the frustration of locating facts and photos, and the joy when they finally do turn up, often when least expected. As mentioned, the Susquehanna's first diesels were only on the property for a very short time before being requisitioned by the government. Given the wartime conditions, we seriously doubted that a photo existed of these two units. But we were to get a double barrelled treat: ABOVE: The first 231 standing at Stillwater station in the summer of 1942. As best can be determined, the first 231 and 233 were delivered in June of that year and it seems that they were on their way back to Schenectady by September or perhaps October, for the first of the rebuilt six-motor units were coming off the line at Alco by November. The second barrel is the train behind the RS1: a special train unloading scouts from the north Jersey area for the trip to their camp on the Delaware River. We were most surprised to find, in talking to Susquehanna oldtimers, that the scout trains were a regular job all through that summer that saw wartime gas rationing imposed. A regular bid job worked a Jersey-Butler commuter run on six days of the week. The seventh day saw them take a scout train from Jersey City to Stillwater with the incoming scouts and return to Jersey City with the boys going home. Although a bus is present in this photo, on most occasions the scouts hiked the six miles from Stillwater to camp. The trains ran through the war, but afterwards the scouts switched over to the Lackawanna, getting off at Blairstown and still hiking the considerable distance.

RIGHT: The Stillwater depot looked surprisingly good in 1961 as an eastbound train passed. By this time, the Susquehanna had adopted the policy of keeping the headlight on in the daytime for improved visibility. The order board is shorn of its blades, for the 69 car passing track west of the station was torn up in the late 1940's and there was no longer a need to write an order at Stillwater.

84

Four L&NE FA freighters smoke it up working east through Marksboro with a train for Maybrook, N.Y. It's the summer of 1961 and in the fall, on the 31st of October, the Lehigh & New England will call it quits. The lead unit sports the simplified paint scheme applied to the FA's while the second unit still has the original stripes on the nose. The L&NE units, like the New York Central lightning stripe engines, seem to be living proof that a plain black and white paint scheme need not be dull looking. The track at the left is the Marksboro station track. The building itself came down in 1937.

Looking the other way, we find another quartet of Alco products on a snowy winter's day in early 1958. The four RS1's are heading west to Hainesburg, following the valley of the Paulins Kill. Slightly east of the station there stood another substantial creamery and a spur, less than a mile in length, led off to White Lake, where ice was harvested for many years. Although coal was the lifeblood of the Susquehanna for many years, it's important to remember that milk, ice, and farm products all added considerable revenue to the balance sheet on the west end of the road.

BELOW: The 705 is looking the worse for wear as it leads three sisters out of Blairstown heading east. It's the fall of 1960 and only another year of operation remains.
ABOVE RIGHT: The view from the Route 94 overhead bridge didn't look all that different ten years earlier in the spring of 1950 as a Susquehanna train went west towards Hainesburg. The Blairstown station is visible on the left in the distance.
BELOW RIGHT: A closer look at the barn like Blairstown station in May 1948 as 252 and 246 lay in the clear waiting for a meet. Blairstown was one of the very few two story station buildings on the entire Susquehanna. In the 1890's, Blairstown had very nearly become an industrial city when a group of Paterson businessmen laid plans to build silk mills. They built a dam on the Kill at Paulina, just east of Blairstown; but a visit by the city fathers to the mills at Stroudsburg disillusioned them sufficiently that the project was never completed. Instead, the dam was used to build a power plant that gave Blairstown a novelty for 1896: electric lights, many years before any of the surrounding communities had electric power. Besides the usual quota of farm products, Blairstown did a particularly heavy passenger business in the old days because of the annual summer influx of vacationers.

JOHN KRAUSE

JOHN L. TREEN

JOHN L. TREEN

Blairstown differed from the other Susquehanna stations west of Butler because it had once been the home of the Blairstown Railway. The 12 mile line was built by John I. Blair, the town's namesake and one of the pioneer New Jersey railroad builders. Blair was involved in the Sussex Railroad, the Lackawanna, and a host of industrial concerns throughout New Jersey and Pennsylvania. The Blairstown Railway was opened in 1877 from Blairstown to a connection with the old main of the Lackawanna at Delaware Station. When the Susquehanna was building west in 1881, they purchased the Blairstown Railway and used the first seven miles to Warrington as the main line and operated the additional five miles as the Delaware branch. The Delaware branch was abandoned in June 1928. In this next sequence of photos, we are going to take a look at a meet between the LNE and the Susquehanna at Blairstown in 1960. John Krause was out chasing both roads and stopping at Swartswood Junction, was informed of the impending meet. The cooperative operator at JU offered to set the meet up at Blairstown or Swartswood Junction, whichever the photographer might prefer, and John opted for Blairstown.

ABOVE: The Lehigh & New England pulls slowly up the main to await the Susquehanna. The open area at the left once contained the turntable and enginehouse of the Blairstown Railway. In the background stands a creamery and across the tracks were coal and lumber sheds, a scale, cattle pens, and a host of support buildings that made Blairstown one of the busiest of the west end S&W stations.

BELOW: The westbound Susquehanna job approaches the east switch of the 70 car passing track. Like most roads, eastbounds were superior by direction, so the S&W will take siding for the eastbound L&NE man.

JOHN KRAUSE

With the Susquehanna safely in the clear, the FA's open up and spew forth the familiar cloud of Alco smoke as they accelerate away from the meet towards their destination at Maybrook. By this time, the once proud Blairstown station had been shorn of its eaves and long since closed. To the uninformed, it might seem to be a barn or a warehouse. Little more than a year remained before the fried egg herald of the L&NE would disappear from the valley of the Paulins Kill.

One of the fixtures on many railroads was the annual employees outing, which usually featured a special train to carry employees to the picnic site. The little Susquehanna was no exception and each summer for many years the picnic train would make its way west to Blairstown Airport. Leaving Jersey City early in the morning, the special would pick up employees at Little Ferry, Paterson, North Hawthorne, and Butler and return late in the day with its cargo of tired and happy excursionists. The first annual Susquehanna Outing, as the trips were known, occurred in 1941, but the war postponed further picnics until 1946. They continued through 1955, but in 1956 the company announced that they couldn't afford to run the train and the annual outings came sadly to an end.

ABOVE: An appropriately decorated 236 stands at the head of the picnic train in the summer of 1951. The crowd unloads and heads for the lake where a large tent was erected and where hot dogs, pop, and beer all fueled a day of swimming, contests, and storytelling among the old-timers. The picnic always brought in many of the old WB&E men from Pennsylvania and we only wish we could be there now to hear the tall stories of the glory days of the Susquehanna.

BELOW: After unloading, the special would run to Hainesburg Junction where the engine would run around the train and lay in the clear until it was time to leave. In this photo, they have come back up from Hainesburg Junction and stopped at the Airport and the frolickers are reluctantly beginning to climb aboard for the trip home. Note that the vintage Stillwells are still in service, but have lost their maroon and gray scheme in favor of a full maroon paint job with only the roof still sporting the gray. The delivery of new Budd coaches in the fall will put the venerable Stillwells out of work for all time.

JOHN L. TREEN

JOHN L. TREEN

Putting 'em down and picking 'em up . . . ABOVE: The Susquehanna was in fine shape in the spring of 1951 and a testimony to their well being is seen here in the form of a gang dropping relay rail at Vails. The 246 and 252 head up the work train and an old tender furnishes the coal supply for the steam crane. The old steam crane was replaced by a new diesel-electric 30 ton crane from American Hoist & Derrick in November 1954. By this time Vails was nothing more than a small sidetrack into a creamery and feed store, for the station had come down in 1938 along with Marksboro. Very old Susquehanna timetables list a station just west of Blairstown known as Kalarama and attempting to find out what became of it produced a rather interesting story. As can best be determined, Kalarama station stood just east of Lake Susquehanna, but of course there was no lake there at that time. Apparently the station didn't pan out and the company decided in 1891 to move it to Vails. You may recall the story of moving the North Hawthorne station by sliding it down the rails. Apparently the road department remembered also and tried the same trick to move Kalarama. This time, instead of trouble with the law, it was the building itself that proved to be trouble. They got it jacked up and moved out on to the rails, but they only slid it for a few hundred feet before it got away from them and tumbled down the bank, smashing into a wonderful pile of kindling wood. Vails apparently got a new station building instead and we can be fairly certain that somebody ended up on the carpet trying to explain what went wrong.

LEFT: In the first few months of 1963, some of this same rail was being pulled back up as the Susquehanna was torn up from Hainesburg Junction to Sparta Junction. In this view, the scrappers are by Vails already and almost into Blairstown. The track was pulled up by the Salzberg interests and at first the scrap train was handled by a GE 70 tonner from Salzberg's Wellsville Addison & Galeton line. Despite the WAG's northern location, the engine froze up and cracked an engine block and the 253 was leased from the Susquehanna to finish the job.

ABOVE: The trees are still bare in the spring of 1950 as 248 and 252 head east to Little Ferry under the graceful arches of the Lackawanna's Paulins Kill viaduct. On the viaduct, a string of reefers rolls along at a good 60 mph clip: one of the Lackawanna's perishable hotshots. The viaduct was the crowning achievement of the construction of the great Lackawanna Cut-Off, completed in 1911 to replace the torturous curves, grades, and tunnels of the old main. At 1100 feet long and 115 feet high, the viaduct was the largest concrete structure in the world until the DL&W beat their own record with the Tunkhannock viaduct in Pennsylvania just a few years later. We've mentioned the fact that the Lehigh & New England actually owned their own right of way from Hainesburg to Swartswood Junctions, but never built upon it in favor of rights over the S&W. When the Cut-Off was constructed, it was incumbent upon the DL&W to protect the LNE's right of way for any future use. This they did by building a stone-arched tunnel under the great fill west of the viaduct near the Route 94 crossing. Although the tunnel has shuddered to the passage of countless Lackawanna trains overhead on the Cut-Off and still feels the daily passage of Conrail, it stands barren and forlorn of ever having had a train pass through its own portals.

JOHN L. TREEN

VINCENT EMMANUEL

JOHN L. TREEN

BELOW LEFT: In this prewar view, Hainesburg station still has its signboard, for the agency had been closed down in 1938. A combination freight and passenger station, Hainesburg was also one of the few two story buildings on the road. Past the station in the distance, tie piles stand where once a thriving creamery had stood.

BELOW RIGHT: In this postwar view, the 246 pulls by the station on the way down to the junction. The station continued to be used by the railroad until 1951, when it was sold to a farm equipment dealer. The weed grown track at the right is the old creamery spur, while the high switchstand by the locomotive controls the east end of a half-mile passing track that extends down to the junction with the L&NE. Despite the proximity of the armstrong turntable at the left to the station, it was not the S&W's, but rather the L&NE's table.

ABOVE LEFT: An unusual sight at the interchange at Hainesburg Junction appears in the summer of 1951 in the form of a string of Stillwell coaches. The company picnic train has come down from Blairstown Airport to run the engine around and lay in wait for the return trip. The picnic train is standing on the old S&W main that once led to the Water Gap, Stroudsburg, and Wilkes-Barre. At the left is a passing track. About a mile of the old main and the passing track were left in

place for switching when the Stroudsburg line was pulled up in 1943. To the right, 248 and 252 are ready to pull their assembled train east off the L&NE main. Note the double train order boards on the diminutive Hainesburg Junction station, one each for the Susquehanna and the Lehigh & New England.

LEFT: In this earlier view, 248 serves as a pusher for an eastbound S&W train; the RS1 is safely tucked away on the old Susquehanna main for the moment because the L&NE will be getting out first. To the right, 252 is teamed up with 246 as the road engines and they too lie in the clear on the No. 1 track of the L&NE yard. The date of this photo is May 2, 1948 and it may well depict the very first road trip of FA's 701 and 702, seen standing on the L&NE main with a drag of coal bound for Maybrook. In the following months, the cab units would continue to be delivered from Schenectady and quickly decimate the L&NE's stable of unusual steam hogs.

ABOVE: The end is near and the once shining paint of the FA's is now tattered and worn as a trio of the Alco's stands at Hainesburg Junction in October 1961, the Lehigh & New England's final month of operation. The brakeman opens the switch in the foreground which leads to the passing track, where the FA's can clear up to allow the Susquehanna to grab their delivery. To the right, an aged sign marks the division point between the two railroads.

RIGHT: A dramatic panorama of Hainesburg Junction taken in the spring of 1950. On the right, an eastbound Susquehanna job stands on the old main while to the left, another westbound train has pulled past the station in the distance and into the L&NE yard to make a delivery. High above on the graceful arches of the Paulins Kill viaduct, the eastbound *Phoebe Snow* streaks across the skyline. So much is gone: the *Phoebe Snow*, the old Lackawanna itself, even the merged Erie-Lackawanna, the Lehigh & New England and the Susquehanna. That enduring monument to Lackawanna engineering - the Paulins Kill viaduct - seems indestructible and bears Conrail freights every day. The viaduct has lost none of its beauty in almost 70 years of service, and the natural beauty of the area around it remains unspoiled; but for the train watcher, the valley of the Paulins Kill has a sad emptiness.

JOHN KRAUSE

JOHN L. TREEN

HOWARD E. JOHNSTON PHOTO, COURTESY WILLIAM S. YOUNG

ABOVE: A quartet of FA's backs across the L&NE's Delaware River bridge in the summer of 1961. The L&NE chose a more frontal assault on the Kittaninny Mountains on the New Jersey side of the river and as a result, were often forced to double their train up the steep grade from the river bridge to Hainesburg yard. The deck girder bridge over the old main of the Lackawanna is partly visible at left, but the similar span over the abandoned Susquehanna roadbed on the New Jersey shore is out of sight at the right. Both the Lackawanna and the L&NE took off from Hainesburg fairly straight towards the west to cross the river, but the Susquehanna followed the tracks of the old Blairstown Railway down to the mouth of the Paulins Kill before turning around and following the river upstream. After crossing under the L&NE bridge, the Susquehanna next went under the graceful concrete arches of the Lackawanna Cut-Off bridge and then considerably upstream past the site of today's I-80 highway bridge before crossing the river and heading for Stroudsburg.
ABOVE RIGHT: The abandoned piers of the NYS&W bridge over the Delaware River in the fall of 1950. In 1955 hurricane Diane would take out the midstream piers. Although some of the piers still stand, the construction of Interstate 80 has obliterated all traces of the S&W roadbed from Columbia to the Water Gap.
RIGHT: The scrappers at work on the line from the Water Gap up to Stroudsburg in 1943. The locomotive is a Vulcan 0-4-0T belonging to a Buffalo scrap firm that ended it's life at the Heidelberg Colliery in Avoca, Pa. The little tank engine didn't have much water capacity so the scrapper rented an Ontario & Western water car, one of two cars built by the O&W in 1942 by mounting old tender tanks on steel framed flat cars. Although the line was torn up to Gravel Place in 1943, a small mile long stretch was left in place from Hainesburg Junction to Warrington station until 1947, when the station track was torn up.

ABOVE: Streamliner 1001 poses for her portrait near the Stroudsburg station on the memorable June 23, 1940 excursion to Gravel Place, back in the days when excursions were strictly a suit and tie affair. Service to Gravel Place officially ended on February 16, 1941 ending almost sixty years of Susquehanna service in the Commonwealth of Pennsylvania, a service begun on October 26, 1882, with the first passenger train to Gravel Place. Service on the Wilkes-Barre & Eastern extension had begun with freights in late 1893 and passenger trains in the first month of 1894. The passenger business never amounted to much and after World War I was handled by a mixed train which was cut off right after the 1937 bankruptcy. One of Walter Kidde's first moves after assuming the Trustee's position was to disavow the lease of the Wilkes-Barre & Eastern, whose losses were made up by the parent Susquehanna under the terms of the lease. Cut loose on its own, the WB&E filed almost simultaneous petitions for bankruptcy and abandonment in September of 1937.

RIGHT: With the abandonment petition already filed, the fate of the WB&E was sealed and the fans came out for one last ride. On June 12, 1938, a special chartered by the New York Division of the Railroad Enthusiasts left Jersey City behind Russian Decapod 2472. In this photo, the special is paused at Shops, eight-tenths of a mile west of Stroudsburg station, where two "Bolsheviks", 2466 and 2428, were put on for the run over the WB&E. The special ran to Suscon, 11 miles short of Wilkes-Barre, and swung on to the Susquehanna Connecting Railroad, which carried them up to Avoca and a connection with the Erie's Wyoming Division for the trip back home. Although billed as a "Farewell to the WB&E" trip, the

excursion was so successful that it was repeated on December 4, 1938. On March 25, 1939, the last WB&E freight train tied up and the Susquehanna's days as a coal road were ended. Today the remains of the Susquehanna Connecting Railroad still survive in the Lackawanna River valley, unused but still in place. The shop buildings at Shops, once a bustling repair center for Camelbacks and Decapods, now serve as the final resting place for junked automobiles.

43

The caboose of an eastbound train rumbles over the Smith's Mills road crossing, framed by the wig-wag crossing signal. This early 1970's photo, taken just before service was cut off west of Butler, brings us up to today and the question of where next? As this book went to press, a hearing was held at which the S&W's major bondholder pressed hard for complete abandonment of the line. In a last minute reprieve, the state of New Jersey stepped in and ordered continued operation until the state can complete a survey of the line's potential.

Human beings have always looked to the past for wisdom and solace and look to the future with hope. Thus we find ourselves in much the same position as the late Walter A. Lucas, whose definitive history of the early Susquehanna was released in 1939, a time when the WB&E was going under, when almost half the trains on the road had been cut, and when Walter Kidde was even publicly considering replacing the whole commuter operation with buses. Lucas had chronicled the great days of the Susquehanna as a coal road and it is doubtful if any of his readers could even imagine what was to come in the years ahead under the stewardship of Kidde and Norton. So we look to the future with hope for the Susquehanna, awash as it is in an increasingly complicated and changing world of railroading. Whatever the future might hold, there can be no doubt that the last forty years of Susquehanna operation have left a mark on the railroad scene that cannot be erased. In a measure disproportionate to its size, the story of our railroads will always have that special chapter entitled simply *Susquehanna*.

RAILFAN: JIM BOYD